SOCIAL INCLUSION
OF PEOPLE WITH DISABILITIES

National and International Perspectives

Social inclusion is often used interchangeably with the terms social cohesion, social integration, and social participation, positioning social exclusion as the opposite. The latter is a contested term that refers to a wide range of phenomena and processes related to poverty and deprivation, but it is also used in relation to marginalized people and places. This book consists of two parts: The first aims to review the domestic and international historical roots and conceptual base of disability, as well as the expressions of social exclusion of people with disabilities that interfere in their efforts to exercise their rights in society. It offers a comprehensive review of social and legal approaches to social exclusion and inclusion. The second part introduces and analyzes domestic and international social and legal strategies to promote social inclusion for people with disabilities. The closing chapter highlights the roles of morality, law, science, and media and technology in achieving social inclusion.

Arie Rimmerman is Richard Crossman Professor of Social Welfare and Social Planning and former Dean of Social Welfare and Health Sciences and Head of the School of Social Work at the University of Haifa, Israel. He is an internationally well-known researcher in social policy and disability who has lectured at several universities in the United States and Europe, including the University of Pennsylvania, Syracuse University, and Charles University in Prague. He has published seven books and hundreds of peer-reviewed articles and research reports in Israel, the United States, Europe, and Australia. He has served as an advisor to ministers of labour and welfare in Israel and public committees on disabilities in Israel, Europe, and the United States. He is the recipient of the Lehman Award (1987), the William Trump Award (1998), the International Award of the American Association on Mental Retardation (1999), and the Burton Blatt Leadership Award (2006).

Cambridge Disability Law and Policy Series

The Cambridge Disability Law and Policy series examines these topics in interdisciplinary and comparative terms. The books in the series reflect the diversity of definitions, causes, and consequences of discrimination against persons with disabilities while illuminating fundamental themes that unite countries in their pursuit of human rights laws and policies to improve the social and economic status of persons with disabilities. The series contains historical, contemporary, and comparative scholarship crucial to identifying individual, organizational, cultural, attitudinal, and legal themes necessary for the advancement of disability law and policy.

The book topics covered in the series also are reflective of the new moral and political commitment by countries throughout the world toward equal opportunity for persons with disabilities in such areas as employment, housing, transportation, rehabilitation, and individual human rights. The series will thus play a significant role in informing policy makers, researchers, and citizens of issues central to disability rights and disability antidiscrimination policies. The series grounds the future of disability law and policy as a vehicle for ensuring that those living with disabilities participate as equal citizens of the world.

Books in the Series:

Ruth Colker, *When Is Separate Unequal? A Disability Perspective*, 2009

Larry M. Logue and Peter Blanck, *Race, Ethnicity, and Disability: Veterans and Benefits in Post–Civil War America*, 2010

Lisa Vanhala, *Making Rights a Reality? Disability Rights Activists and Legal Mobilization*, 2010

Alicia Ouellette, *Bioethics and Disability: Toward a Disability-Conscious Bioethics*, 2011

Eilionoir Flynn, *From Rhetoric to Action: Implementing the UN Convention on the Rights of Persons with Disabilities*, 2011

Isabel Karpin and Kristin Savell, *Perfecting Pregnancy: Law, Disability, and the Future of Reproduction*, 2012

Arie Rimmerman, *Social Inclusion of People with Disabilities: National and International Perspectives*, 2013

Andrew Power, Janet E. Lord, and Allison S. deFranco, *Active Citizenship & Disability: Implementing the Personalisation of Support for Persons with Disabilities*, 2012

Eliza Varney, *Disability and Information Technology: A Comparative Study in Media Regulation*, 2013

Social Inclusion of People with Disabilities

NATIONAL AND INTERNATIONAL PERSPECTIVES

Arie Rimmerman
University of Haifa

CAMBRIDGE
UNIVERSITY PRESS

32 Avenue of the Americas, New York NY 10013-2473, USA

Cambridge University Press is part of the University of Cambridge.

It furthers the University's mission by disseminating knowledge in the pursuit of education, learning and research at the highest international levels of excellence.

www.cambridge.org
Information on this title: www.cambridge.org/9781107415294

© Arie Rimmerman 2013

First published 2013
First paperback edition 2014

A catalogue record for this publication is available from the British Library

Library of Congress Cataloguing in Publication data

Rimmerman, Arie.
Social inclusion of people with disabilities : national and international perspectives / Arie Rimmerman.
  p.   cm. – (Cambridge disability law and policy series)
Includes bibliographical references and index.
ISBN 978-1-107-01462-6 (hardback : alk. paper)
1. People with disabilities – Social conditions.   2. People with disabilities – Legal status, laws, etc.   3. Social integration.   I. Title.
HV1568.R56   2013
305.9′08–dc23   2012032216

ISBN 978-1-107-01462-6 Hardback
ISBN 978-1-107-41529-4 Paperback

To my wife, Shula Rimmerman, for her love, compassion, and wisdom

CONTENTS

FOREWORD

It is my great pleasure to write the foreword to this book. It has been remarked that persons with disabilities – especially those with intellectual disabilities – are just emerging from a form of 'civil death' throughout the world. Instead of being regarded as 'objects' to be managed or cared for, they are finally being acknowledged and treated as autonomous human 'subjects' in their own right. Of course we are all agreed about the need to move from 'object' to 'subject'. But that begs the question What does it mean to be a human subject?

It turns out that morality, law, and science intersect positively on this core question. From a moral point of view, we are all agreed that personhood is not something experienced in isolation but is in fact shared and best developed in community. From a legal point of view, we now have an innovative right to live independently and be included in the community under international law – a useful conjunction of two seemingly separate ideals. And contemporary neuroscience emphasises the extent to which the mind is a 'relational' idea – an ideal that is best nourished in community. Building bridges between people holds the key to human flourishing in general and particularly in the context of intellectual disability where the 'mystic cords of memory' that connect people have been shattered through needless isolation and segregation. For a long time these deep questions about personhood and flourishing could be – and were – ignored. They certainly did not figure prominently in any of the existing UN human rights treaties, which focus more on power and the intersection of the individual and the State. But they simply could not be avoided in the drafting of the landmark UN Convention on the Rights of Persons with Disabilities (UN CRPD).

Taking personhood seriously is the leitmotiv of the UN CRPD. That is why it seeks to restore power to people with disabilities over their own lives through reform of legal incapacity laws throughout the world. And that is why the convention is now emblazoned with a headline provision on the right to live independently and be included in the community – something that requires a revolution in how services are imagined and delivered. Indeed, it is probably fair to say that we really do need to break away from the language of 'needs' and 'services' and begin reflecting more intensively on how services can truly subserve the higher goal of enabling people to live the life they want and become much more directly accountable to these people. None of this will happen unless a way can be found to unlock resources currently tied up in institutions to better serve people in the community and through generally accessible community services. But maybe the biggest challenge of all – the one that can pay most dividends if handled correctly – will be to reconnect people to the naturally occurring social capital in their own communities. And this won't happen unless popularly portrayed images of people with disabilities change. The need to do so is both a moral imperative and also a precondition for successful inclusion. Indeed, the CRPD also requires States to 'nurture receptiveness to the rights of persons with disabilities'.

The value of this book is that it probes the problematic nature of social exclusion experienced by persons with disabilities; it explores what living independently and living in the community actually mean and it takes analysis to the next level of examining strategies and means for the achievement of inclusion. In its own way it contributes to the worldwide debate and process of ending 'civil death' and finding innovative ways of ensuring the human flourishing of the individual in community regardless of disability. This book has global significance as all countries take the next step to implement the right to live independently and be included in the community. It continues the great humanitarian tradition of Stanley Herr and keeps his memory alive in the best possible way – by pointing to new ways of extending the blessings of freedom to all.

Gerard Quinn
Galway, Ireland

PREFACE

This book is my conceptual review and search for national and international perspectives of social inclusion and disability. Social inclusion has numerous interpretations with respect to people with disabilities. Most of the researchers define social inclusion in relation to social exclusion and believe that they are actually two sides of the same coin. However, there are also other interpretations that do not see the two on the same continuum and prefer to see them separately. Social scientists have the tendency to express social inclusion in terms of social or economic measures, arguing that it is actually dependent on availability of adequate resources or conditions. If there is lack of such resources, there is a need to provide them. Legal scholars see social inclusion as a human rights issue and call for antidiscrimination policies or equal opportunity legislation. This book offers my interpretation as an international researcher who has been involved in the disability area for more than three decades.

My interest in writing this book began in the early 2000s after completing with Stanley Herr research of the disability strike in Israel in 2000. Our article, which analysed portrayals of the first major disability strike as it appeared in the printed media, pointed out that the public held traditional stereotypes of people with disabilities despite their growing awareness of the new disability rights legislation of 1998.[1]

---

[1] See Arie Rimmerman and Stanley Herr, 'The power of the powerless: A study of the 2000's disability strike in Israel', *Journal of Disability Policy Studies* 15 (2004), 12–18. Professor Stan Herr died in 2001 and the article was completed after his death. He was a University of Maryland law professor who, for nearly two decades, taught civil rights, human rights, and clinical legal education.

In 2005, I initiated the first Israeli study on social and civic participation of people with disabilities as compared to those without disabilities using international comparable instrumentation.[2] The results confirmed my earlier impression that compared to people without disabilities, people with disabilities experienced significantly lower social and civic participation rates and felt that the primary obstacles were social exclusion and the lack of economic resources. This national research encouraged me to explore social and legal strategies to promote social inclusion of people with disabilities.

Two years later, I was fortunate to be involved in the Digital Freedom Project in Norway with other international experts including Rune Halvorsen, Bjorn Hvinden, Gerard Quinn, and Peter Blanck.[3] The project addressed the importance of international policies geared towards e-Accessibility and e-Inclusion of people with disabilities. It demonstrated not only the potential of information and communications technology (ICT) to citizens in Europe and the United States but also the concerns of whether the available technological facilities, products, and services are usable by all people and whether ICT could provide the necessary and appropriate adjustments of the social environment to meet the needs of individuals with disabilities.

I began writing the book proposal after being invited by the S.I. Newhouse School of Public Communications to teach a graduate course on 'Mass Media and Disability'. This course provides an overview of the literature and research on mass media and disabilities with a focus on analysis of images of people with disabilities as reflected in television, radio, newspapers, and films, and the changes that have occurred in disability imagery over the years. The course provided an insightful look at the sources of social exclusion as they appeared in images and stereotypes of people with disabilities in the United States.

This book explores the historical roots of social exclusion of people with disabilities, conceptualisation of social inclusion, expressions of

---

[2] Arie Rimmerman, Tal Araten-Bergman, and Avi Griffel, *Social participation of people with and without disabilities* (Haifa, Israel: University of Haifa, Social Welfare and Health Sciences, 2006).

[3] The project was funded by the Research Council of Norway, The Welfare Research Program (Grant No. 172472/S20).

images and stereotypes, and appearance in the print and digital media. Furthermore, it provides a critical analysis of domestic and global social and legal strategies used to increase social inclusion of people with disabilities.

Arie Rimmerman
Haifa, Israel

ACKNOWLEDGMENTS

This book was made possible by generous support from my research staff at the Richard Crossman Chair of Social Welfare and Social Planning at the University of Haifa. I am grateful to two scholars who passed away a decade ago – Professors Gunnar Dybwad and Stanley S. Herr – for their legacy. Gunnar taught me during my doctoral studies in the late 1970s and early 1980s that we must better understand our own history in order to make an impact on the present. I follow Gunnar's recommendation by exploring the historical roots of social exclusion of people with disabilities and their relevance to current strategies for promoting social inclusion. Stan was a great believer in human rights and disability rights and thought that Americans could not only contribute but could also learn a lot from their exposure to different international legislation and policies. I have been inspired by his views by offering domestic and international strategies for promoting social inclusion.

I would like to thank my colleagues with whom I informally discussed some of the ideas examined in the book. Finally, I am grateful to my family for facilitating this important project; they have been of tremendous support to me.

1 INTRODUCTION

The term *social inclusion* is often interchangeably used by policy makers and professionals to mean social cohesion, social integration and social participation, or as the opposite term to *social exclusion*. It seems that the latter is a contested term referring to a wide range of phenomena and processes related to poverty, deprivation and hardship but it is also used in relation to a wide range of categories of marginalised people and places. There is no doubt that the term requires refinement and a tighter conceptual base.[1]

A meta-analysis of the use of social inclusion in qualitative disability studies found six common expressions: (1) being accepted and recognised as an individual beyond the disability; (2) having personal relationships with family, friends and acquaintances; (3) being involved in recreation, leisure and other social activities; (4) having appropriate living accommodation; (5) having employment and (6) having appropriate formal and informal support.[2]

The book has two parts; the first part (Chapters 2–4) aims to review the historical roots and conceptual base of disability and the expressions of social exclusion of people with disabilities, which interfere in their efforts to exercise their rights in society. In addition, it offers a comprehensive review of social and legal approaches to social exclusion and inclusion. The second part (Chapters 5–8) introduces and analyses domestic and international social and legal strategies to promote social inclusion for people with disabilities. The core strategies – which include social

---

[1] Robin Peace, 'Social exclusion: A concept in need of definition?' *Social Policy Journal of New Zealand* 16 (2001), 17–35.

[2] Sarah A. Hall, 'The social inclusion of people with disabilities: A qualitative meta-analysis', *Journal of Ethnographic and Qualitative Research* 3 (2009), 162–73. Hall provides a rare attempt to define social inclusion from the perspective of persons with a disability.

protection, amending discriminatory laws and national and international campaigns geared toward removal of stigmas and barriers – need public consensus and support. The underlying rationale is that there is interrelation between the in-depth understanding of the exclusion process and adopting effective and evidence-based strategies to remove barriers and promote social inclusion. Chapter 9 provides closing remarks about the roles of biblical, theological and historical perspectives in the analysis of preferred strategies for promoting social inclusion.

Chapter 2 offers an in-depth history of disability with themes that embrace notions of sin, impurity and wholeness, undesirability and weakness, and care and compassion. Surprisingly, substantial stereotypes and prejudice toward people with disabilities today were imported from Ancient Greece and Rome, from demonology and witchcraft of the Middle Ages and from the modern period.

The conceptualisation of disability is based on the early modern period and the rise of the eugenic and medicalisation approaches associated with social welfare policies. The heart of this section is understanding the transition from the medical model to the social functional model of disability, which is also connected with shifting from social welfare to human rights legislation and policies. There is a direct linkage between adopting social and human rights models and the hope that people with disabilities will be better integrated into society.

It is surprising that the terms *social inclusion* and *social exclusion* are used frequently in the field without recognising their conceptual and theoretical bases. The first part of Chapter 3 explores general expressions of social exclusion, its European roots, definitions and multidimensionality, which reflect an overlap with poverty, employment, economic distress and lack of social capital and social participation.[3] There is an interesting debate about the paradigms and whether social inclusion and social exclusion are inseparable sides of the same coin or are separate concepts. There is an interesting discussion about the interrelations between the two terms and social capital, stigma and their standardised measures.

The second part of this book is an effort to demonstrate and discuss how social exclusion and social inclusion are interpreted in the disability

---

[3] Robert Putnam, 'Who killed civil America?' *Prospect* 7 (1996), 66–72.

scene. There are three illustrations that demonstrate domestic and international indicators taken from the Kessler Foundation and the National Organization on Disability Report of 2010;[4] the Leonard Cheshire Disability report of 2008;[5] and the 2003 cross-country study of social inclusion in Organisation for Economic Co-operation and Development (OECD) countries.[6] There is also an introduction of non-indicator approaches taken from other countries, including the UK and Israel. It is evident that there is an interrelationship between historical roots and conceptualisation of disability (Chapter 1), expressions and processes of social exclusion (Chapter 3), and how the media construct the current images of disability. Chapter 4 demonstrates the role of the printed, and particularly the digital, media in shaping public attitudes and impressions of people with disabilities. Special attention has been given to the paradoxical and unintentional impacts of classical literature, Hollywood films and advertising campaigns on their inclusion in the domestic arena and in other countries.

Attention is also given to two issues that may play an important role in social inclusion of people with disabilities – *disability culture* and *digital divide*. The discussion of *disability culture* demonstrates that the efforts of people with disabilities to strengthen and keep their unique identities may hamper their ability to integrate into non-disabled society. An interesting example presented in the chapter is of the deaf culture and the threat of cochlear implants to their identity. *Digital divide* is another example of how lack of accessibility in design, development and production of telecommunication services and products and digital literacy can prevent a substantial number of people with disabilities from achieving social inclusion. Chapter 5 is based on social exclusion conceptualisation (Chapter 3) and offers overall economic and social strategies that have been proven to combat poverty for people with disabilities. These strategies are discussed with respect to their relevance and merit to people with disabilities. There is a critical discussion about social protection provisions, which trade self-sufficiency for a tendency to strengthen dependency and

---

[4] Kessler Foundation and National Organization on Disability/NOD, *The ADA, 20 years later: Survey of Americans with disabilities* (New York: Harris Interactive, 2010).

[5] Leonard Cheshire, *Disability poverty in the UK* (London: Leonard Cheshire, 2008).

[6] OECD, *Transforming disability into ability: Policies to promote work and income security for disabled people* (Paris: OECD, 2003).

segregation. Another strategy that is discussed is social capital, with a reservation regarding whether it is relevant for certain subpopulations. Chapter 6 discusses whether disability rights legislation can promote social exclusion and replace discrimination practices. It examines this question by reviewing and testing three national legislations[7] and studies their impact on social inclusion practice. The 1990 Americans with Disabilities Act (ADA) was the milestone for other foreign disability rights legislation. The chapter therefore analyses in depth the required changes needed in this human rights legislation, which may lead to comparable changes in other countries.

Chapter 7 is an examination of the international legal strategy that introduces and analyses the first human rights treaty of the twenty-first century: the United Nations (UN) Convention on the Rights of Persons with Disabilities (CRPD).[8] The central question discussed is whether an international legal instrument based on the social model of disability can enhance social inclusion of people with disabilities domestically and globally. Specifically, the CRPD has gone beyond the ADA and similar disability rights legislation and calls for protection of basic rights and adequate standards of living. The chapter examines the potential of such a maximalist international law to be transferred to domestic policy, legislation and domestic courts by presenting two illustrations from Europe and Israel regarding Article 19. Chapter 8 introduces and discusses national and international strategies to promote positive images of people with disabilities in the media and whether narrowing the digital divide can enhance their social inclusion in society. The strategies discussed in terms of their merits and shortcomings include macro interventions such as guidelines for adequately portraying people with disabilities in the media and Web accessibility, implementation of Article 8 of the UN CRPD and media campaigns taken from Europe and Australia that aim to improve images of people with disabilities. There are also micro-strategies that address special issues, such as the United States'

---

[7] See the Americans with Disabilities Act of 1990/2008, the UK Disability Discrimination Act of 1995/2010 and Israel's 1998 Equal Rights for Persons with Disabilities Law.

[8] The United Nations (UN) Convention on the Rights of Persons with Disabilities (CRPD) was adopted by the UN General Assembly on December 13, 2006, and came into force on May 3, 2008.

The Kids on the Block[9] educational TV programme, progressive advertising and recognising successful media practices that are discussed with respect to their positive impact on children and the public. Finally, the chapter provides an overview and discussion of the United States and Europe, documenting solutions of bridging the digital divide for people with disabilities. In addition, it offers evidence-based practices with recommendations to increase access to and use for vulnerable targeted groups.

Chapter 9 provides closing remarks and insights regarding social exclusion and strategies to promote social inclusion. The author tries to highlight and respond briefly to core questions related to social inclusion of people with disabilities nationally and internationally. He asks: What is the impact of biblical, theological and historical perspectives on current views of inclusion of people with disabilities? Which strategy is more effective in promoting social inclusion of people with disabilities: social or legal? Can the media change portrayals of people with disabilities? Is it possible to narrow the digital divide? The answers reflect the importance of developing interdisciplinary knowledge and collaboration among people and nations in challenging social exclusion and promoting social inclusion for people with disabilities.

---

[9] *The Kids on the Block*, a U.S. programme that spreads awareness about disabilities, was started in 1977 by a special education teacher; the show features puppets that have cerebral palsy, epilepsy, spina bifida, autism, muscular dystrophy and more. The curricula cover a variety of topics related to disabilities such as medical and social concerns.

Part 1   SOCIAL INCLUSION AND DISABILITY

2   HISTORICAL ROOTS AND CONCEPTUALISING DISABILITY

We cannot understand disability today without knowing the way that humanity treated people with physical and mental impairments through-out history.[1] Henri-Jacques Stiker, the director of research and member of the department of the History and Civilization of Western Societies, University of Paris VII, believes that the clues are hidden in Judeo-Christian and Greco-Roman roots – particularly, in the Bible and ancient, medieval and modern times. A historical perspective can provide in-depth analysis as to how society accommodates and handles people with disabilities, thus providing an insightful look at ourselves and whether we have learned lessons from our past. This chapter provides a brief and thought-provoking review of the status of people with disabilities and the changes that have occurred in the conceptualisation of disability from the eugenic movement to modern times.

LEARNING FROM HISTORY: THE BIBLE, THE NEW TESTAMENT AND THE QUR'AN

Persons with disabilities have always been *in* but not *part of* society. Their vague and unclear social standing in ancient society is reflected in the Bible, the New Testament and the Qur'an. Leviticus,[2] the third book of the Torah,[3] protects the well-being of the deaf and the blind by commanding: 'Thou shalt not curse the deaf nor put a stumbling block before the blind, nor maketh the blind to wander out of [his] path'.[4]

---

[1] Henri-Jacques Stiker, *History of disability* (Ann Arbor: University of Michigan Press, 2000), pp. 1–5.
[2] In Hebrew, Vayikra.
[3] The Five Books of Moses in the Bible.
[4] Lev., 19:4.

However, in the same book it is written that:

> The Lord spoke further to Moses: Speak to Aaron and say: No man of
> your offspring throughout the ages who has a defect shall be qualified
> to offer the food of his God. No one at all who has a defect shall be
> qualified: no man who is blind, or lame, or has a limb too short or
> too long; no man who has a broken leg or a broken arm; or who is a
> hunchback, or a dwarf, or who has a growth in his eye, or who has a
> boil-scar, or scurvy, or crushed testes. No man among the offspring of
> Aaron the priest who has a defect shall be qualified to offer the Lord's
> offering by fire; having a defect, he shall not be qualified to offer the
> food of his God. He may eat of the food of his God, of the most holy
> as well as of the holy; but he shall not enter behind the curtain or come
> near the altar, for he has a defect. He shall not profane these places
> sacred to Me, for I the Lord have sanctified them.[5]

Is it possible that the Bible presents such an ambivalent approach, recognising the obligation to remove barriers from blind people but by the same
token prevents them from serving the Lord? It appears that the Bible
reflects the common approach that was prevalent at that time regarding
the code of purity and holiness – namely, that every *kohen* (priest) who
suffered a physical blemish was disqualified by virtue of his disability
from performing the sacrificial ritual. Although the text does not explain
the rationale behind this exclusion, it is clear that a blemished priest was
regarded as unholy, because he was forbidden to eat from the holy food in
the holy portions. This distinguished persons with disabilities from their
colleagues, treating them as totally unfit to carry out the priestly tasks or
share in the priestly emoluments.

Although the text reflects exclusion of people with disabilities, the
Bible's approach seems relatively more progressive than the common
voices in the Greco-Roman world, which advocated infanticide and
euthanasia for people with disabilities.

A similar interpretation about the biblical approach toward disability
was offered by Rabbi Judith Abrams in her book *Judaism and Disability*.[6]
She argued that the Temple was a place of liminality, where heaven and

---

[5] Lev., 21:16–23.
[6] Judith Z. Abrams, *Judaism and disability: Portrayals in ancient texts from the Tanach through the Bavli* (Washington, D.C.: Galludet University Press, 1998), pp. 104–12.

earth, mortality and immortality, purity and imperfection, all met. Liminal places were dangerous, and therefore the kohen had to be healthy, strong and pure in order to serve. However, this traditional explanation fails to explain why a kohen who is functionally fit cannot officiate at the Temple because he has a scar.

Leviticus's approach to disability is not different from other sources in the Bible. For example, the Bible tends to be protective toward people with blindness, describing them as dependent and helpless[7] or vulnerable to exploitation by the general public.[8] The message is clear: Because they cannot cope with society and are in need of protection from harm, the Bible warns against taking advantage of them.[9]

The impression that the Bible is prejudiced against people with disability was an uneasy one for some interpreters. Therefore, some took the position that exclusion indicated that at one time they were forbidden entrance to the temples.[10] There are several metaphoric meanings to blindness in the Bible, from being dumb to morally unfit.[11] Judges are warned that bribes or gifts blind the eyes of the discerning.[12] Isaiah is told that his mission is to cloud the eyes of Israel so that it will not 'see' and consequently repent and be healed.[13] It is imperative that the Bible views blindness as a body defect, sometimes caused by the Lord and sometimes pitied by him.

However, the Bible is less clear about people with mental illness. For example, among the curses threatened for faithlessness to the covenant is 'so that thou shalt be mad [*meshuggah*] for the sake of thine eyes which thou shalt see'.[14] Other illustrations depict King Saul, who was terrified by an evil spirit. David was invited to play the harp for him so that he could find relief[15] and feigned madness when he fled to the court of Achish, the king of Gath.[16] A midrashic interpretation is that David questions why

---

[7] Sam. II, 5:6; Isa., 35:5–6; Jer., 31:7.
[8] Deut., 28:29.
[9] Lev., 19:14; Deut., 27:18; Job, 29:15.
[10] Sam. II, 5:8.
[11] Isa., 29:9–10, 18.
[12] Ex., 23:8; Deut., 16:19.
[13] Isa., 6:10.
[14] Deut., 28:34.
[15] Sam. I, 16:14–23.
[16] See Sam. I, 21:13–16; Psalms, 31:1.

God would have created such a purposeless state as insanity. But when he saves his life by pretending to be mad, David understands that madness also has a purpose. However, the term is often used differently. Hosea, the prophet, is ironically described as 'mad'.[17]

A similar traditional approach toward people with disabilities existed in the early Christian Church, as they were partially allowed to take part in religious ceremonies. The rejection was toward those with inability to hear, or their perceived religious activities.[18] Although the New Testament held similar views as the Bible regarding blindness, the interpretation of this impairment went beyond that: Jesus healed a number of blind people.[19] There are two examples that interpret blind people as sinners in need of cure. Bartimaeus looked for the restoration of his sight from Jesus, who told him 'Your faith has made you whole'.[20] In John, Jesus explained that 'It was not this man sinned or his parents, but that the works of God might made manifest in him'.[21] These healing stories emphasised the supernatural etiology of blindness and that this impairment, as well as others, can be curable.

It appears that early Christianity was compassionate to the needy, the sick and the disabled who were portrayed as sinners or as related to sin. Jesus' magical ability to cure the sick and people with disabilities symbolises his special power over evil. Wolf Wolfensberger thought that the seeds of neglect and rejection of disability were sown in the early days of the Christian Church.[22] In this respect, the church was as vulnerable to the same human and social dynamics as other social institutions.

Does Islam adopt a similar view toward people with disabilities as the Judeo-Christian one? In general, the Qur'an, revealed by Prophet Muhammad in the sixth century AD, views disability in a broad sense. The closest interpretation of disability is among disadvantaged conditions that are created in society.[23] They are reflected as an inability to fulfill

---

[17] Hosea, 9:7.
[18] Rom., 10:17.
[19] Matt., 9:27–28; 12:22; 15:30–1; 21:14.
[20] Mark, 10:15.
[21] John, 9:3.
[22] Wolf Wolfensberger, 'An attempt toward a theology of social integration of devalued/ handicapped people', *Information Service* 8 (1979), 12–26.
[23] Maysaa S. Bazna and Tarek A. Hatab, 'Disability in the Qur'an', *Journal of Religion, Disability & Health* 9 (2008). Available at http://hatworthpress.com/web/JRDH.

social, economic or physical norms. In a fairly recent study, Maysaa S. Bazna and Tarek A. Hatab listed two groups of disadvantaged conditions associated with disability in the Qur'an.[24] The first is described as physical conditions and perceived as neither a curse nor a blessing. These afflicted people can be relieved from certain commands and requirements because of their burden. The second group relates to those who cannot measure up in cultural, social and economic life. People of this group often experience social exclusion and ignorance. While the Qur'an calls for social responsibility and obligation toward these people, the call is generic and does not relate to a specific impairment or disability.

ANCIENT GREECE AND ROME

The ancient Greece philosophers Aristotle and Plato were the first to discuss eugenics.[25] The Greeks viewed reality as consisting of physical, mental and social well-being, and separated the good from the beautiful and individual value from submission to the community. It was imperative that they accepted the idea of eugenics as a reflection of their views about the state, both referring to the city-state's need for healthy citizens to form an elite ruling class and army. Men and women were encouraged to reproduce when they were at the peak of their physical and mental powers in order to conceive the healthiest and most intelligent children. The next step was infanticide (the killing of newborn infants), practised in Sparta for deformed newborns; those predicted as being incapable of self-sufficiency and integration into society were subject to immediate death.[26]

Ancient Greece (and later Rome) used people with disabilities as objects of mockery in social and sport events, as in the case of the Hephaestus's Olympian feast. Greece vase paintings depict 'hunchbacks, cripples, dwarfs and obese women' performing as entertainers. In addition, Greek mythology portrayed disability as a punishment, as in the case of Teiresias who was blinded because he saw Athena bathing, though he was compensated by his remarkable abilities. The ancient Greeks

---

[24] Ibid.
[25] David J. Galton, 'Greek theories on eugenics', *Journal of Medical Ethics* 24 (1998), 263–7.
[26] Plutarch, 'Lycurgus'. In *Greek lives*. Edited by Philip A. Stadter, translated by Robin Water-field (Oxford: Oxford University Press, 1998), pp. 3–41.

believed that blind people could develop exceptional sensory perception and insights. Aristotle thought that the blind remembered better, being released from having their faculty of memory engaged with objects of sight.[27]

Although the Romans were not different from their predecessors in practising social exclusion and marginalisation of people with disabilities, they were the first to offer them some legal support. Early Roman law protected the property rights of people with intellectual disabilities, offering them guardians to assist and manage their affairs.[28] This important law authorised deaf people capable of speech to integrate into civic and social society. They could get married, own property and make decisions about their personal and economic life. Later Roman law was even more progressive as the Justinian code classified persons with disabilities according to the severity of their disability. This piece of legislation became the infrastructure of law in most European countries from the sixth to the eighteenth century.

To sum up, ancient history reflects a mix of and paradoxical approach toward people with disabilities. The Bible, for example, expresses dual and ambivalent views of people with disabilities. On the one hand, it was considered immoral to prevent them from access to daily activities, but at the same time it excluded them from officiating in certain religious services because they were considered to be less holy. The New Testament offers both redemption opportunities for kind strangers and signifying superstition. Similarly, Ancient Greece and Rome offered contradictory interpretations of disability, from killing of newborns with congenital disabilities to quite progressive legislation for people with disabilities in Rome.

THE MIDDLE AGES

The Middle Ages are characterised by mixed and contradictory views toward people with disabilities. They are portrayed as excluded human beings, demons involved in witchcraft, but also as pitiful and in need

---

[27] Aristotle, *Eudemian ethics* (English), p. 1248a.
[28] Margret A. Winzer, *The history of special education: From isolation to integration* (Washington, D.C.: Gallaudet University Press, 1993), pp. 6–37.

of mercy and charitable services.[29] The most prevalent belief was that people with disabilities were supernatural, devils and witches.[30] In this context, epilepsy, as well as psychotic episodes, was perceived as curable by exorcism and religious rituals. France is a very good example of a country that, led primarily by the Catholic Church, witnessed executions of witches. Parallel to the demonisation of people with disabilities, churches and pilgrimages arranged shelters for these victims until they would be cured.

The twelfth century marked the beginning of a societal organisational response to excluded people, such as building quarantines for people with leprosy. In the thirteenth century, Germany opened the first asylums for people with mental illness. However, these institutions received very little care and the true purpose was the protection of the community. There is no doubt that people with disabilities, and in particularly those with strange or visibly odd appearance or behaviour, were excluded from any social participation.

EARLY MODERN PERIOD THROUGH THE EIGHTEENTH CENTURY

The Renaissance marked a significant change in the status of people with special needs in society. This progressive period shaped the relationship between humans, society and God, and called for the provision of special care for people with mental illness, epilepsy and sensory impairments.[31] However, institutional response reflected the values of the time and offered only segregated care, remote from society. For example, legal records in England in the eighteenth century disclosed debates as to whether their role was the safety of people with disabilities or the protection of society from danger. The debate reflects the social exclusion of people with disabilities as they were judged based on the impact they had on their local communities.[32]

---

[29] Irina Metzler, *Disability in medieval Europe: Thinking about physical impairment in the high Middle Ages, c. 1100–c. 1400* (London: Routledge, 2006; 2010), pp. 38–64.

[30] Franz G. Alexander and Sheldon T. Selesnick, *The history of psychiatric thoughts and practice from prehistoric times to the present* (New York: Harper & Row, 1964), pp. 18–20.

[31] Sander L. Gilman, *Seeing the insane* (New York: Wiley, 1982).

[32] Peter Rushton, 'Lunatics and idiots: Mental disability, the community, and the poor law in North-East England, 1600–1800', *Medical History* 32 (1988), 34–50.

The modern period is further characterised by the development of scientific knowledge. In 1605, Bacon published his book *The Advancement of Learning*, which predicted that the core progress in years to come would be the interaction between body and mind and the individual and society.[33] This uncommon perspective contributed to medicalisation and the placement of people with intellectual and psychiatric disabilities in segregated institutional facilities.[34] The nineteenth and twentieth centuries were marked by expansion of institutional care in Europe and the United States.

THE NINETEENTH CENTURY

The nineteenth and twentieth centuries revealed the problematic and marginalised status of people with disabilities in society. There was significant and positive development in education and care; programmes were provided in segregated institutional settings, justifying the benefits of receiving special services distant from the community.[35] These conflicting forces received support from the eugenics movement which sought to strengthen society by encouraging people with a 'goodly heritage' to bear children, while those with a history of 'defectives' in the family were discouraged from reproducing. The early nineteenth century was characterised by the rapid growth of special and segregated residential schools for children with physical and sensory disabilities in Europe. The best-known developments were braille for the blind and programmatic innovations in deafness and intellectual disabilities.

The rise of institutional care is attributed to urbanisation, manufacturing and changing demographics, including massive immigration. However, there is disagreement among social historians in the United States about the appearance of institutions at the beginning of the nineteenth century. Were they expanded as a rapid response to significant

---

[33] See Francis Bacon, *The advancement of learning*. Edited by Michael Kiernan (Oxford: Oxford University Press, 2000).

[34] Gershon Berkson and Steven J. Taylor, 'Intellectual and physical disabilities in prehistory and early civilization', *Mental Retardation* 42 (2004), 195–208.

[35] David Braddock and Susan Parish, 'An institutional history of disability'. In *Handbook of disability studies*. Edited by Gary L. Albrecht, Katherine D. Seelman and Michael Bury (New York: Sage, 2001), pp. 11–68.

and overwhelming social and economic changes in American society or to the need to control deviant members of a growing society?[36] The answer is probably both, namely that progress created more pressure on society to offer solutions but also to control and monitor those placed in these settings.

A thorough investigation of institutionalisation in the United States reveals that most of the institutions were established in the Northeast followed by the opening of state institutions in other areas.[37] Advocates of the time called for the transition of people with mental illness from prisons and their families to special institutional care facilities.[38] The expansion of custodial institutions was a fairly late development: In 1900, there were twenty-five facilities in the United States, most of them built as segregated and remote entities, detached from their communities.

THE FIRST HALF OF THE TWENTIETH CENTURY: EUGENICS AND THE EXPANSION OF INSTITUTIONALISATION

The period between the late nineteenth century and the middle of the twentieth century was under the influence of eugenics. The term was defined by Francis Galton as the science of the 'well born'.[39] In his words,

> Man is gifted with pity and other kindly feelings; he has also the power of preventing many kinds of suffering. I conceive it to fall well within his province to replace Natural Selection by other processes that are more merciful and not less effective . . . Natural Selection rests upon excessive production and wholesale destruction; Eugenics on bringing no more individuals into the world than can be properly cared for, and those only of the best stock.[40]

Galton's ideas were eventually assimilated into a movement that also relied on the laws of heredity formulated in 1860 by Gregor Mendel, and which

---

[36] David J. Rothman, *The discovery of the asylum: Social order and disorder in the new republic* (Hawthorne, NY: Aldine De Gruyter, 2002).

[37] Braddock and Parish, 'An institutional history of disability', 31–3.

[38] See Dorothea Dix's writing memorials at Brown, 1998.

[39] Francis Galton coined the term 'eugenics' in 1883.

[40] Francis Galton, *Memories of my life* (London: Methuen, 1908), pp. 32–3.

became widely noticed only in the first decade of the twentieth century.[41] The national movement was obsessed with the search for the 'better baby' and the identification of the bearers of 'germ plasm', the eugenic term for what is today known as DNA. The energies of the movement turned to negative eugenics expressed by 'racial integrity' laws to prevent interracial marriage and by euthanasia of the 'defective newborn'.[42] Eugenic ideology used popular mythologies such as the inferior Jukes (inherited criminality) and Kallikaks (inherited intellectual disability) families. These families were socially excluded, and were presented as lower species of humankind and the cause of feeblemindedness and sexual excesses.[43]

The most popular means of 'cleaning up the gene pool', and the one with the most widespread legal mandates in the United States, was eugenic sterilisation.[44] The first sterilisation law was enacted in Indiana in 1907, and for twenty years another twelve states passed their own eugenics laws.[45] The constitutional status of the sterilisation law was examined in the case of *Buck v. Bell*.[46] Carrie Buck, a young Virginia woman whose family history was presented as inferior in terms of hereditary moral degeneracy for three generations, was the subject of a Supreme Court case, which tested the 1924 Virginia sterilisation law.[47] The shameful Supreme Court decision, which upheld the Virginia sterilisation law, proved how deeply rooted eugenics ideology was in American society. The ruling, written by senior Justice Oliver Wendell Holmes, Jr., stated: 'It is better for the world, if instead of waiting to execute degenerate offspring for crime, or to let them starve for their imbecility, society can

---

[41] Paul A. Lombardo, *Eugenic sterilization laws*, Image Archive, American Eugenics Movement (February 2000). Available at http://www.eugenicsarchive.org/eugenics/list3.pl.

[42] For a comprehensive review, see Paul A. Lombardo (Ed.), *A century of eugenics in America: From the Indiana experiment to the human genome* (Bloomington, IN: Indiana University Press, 2011).

[43] For a complete coverage of these families, see Nicole Hahn Rafter, *White trash: The eugenic family studies, 1877–1919* (Boston: Northeastern University Press, 1988).

[44] Paul A. Lombardo, 'Human sterilization'. In *International encyclopedia of the social sciences*, 2nd edition. Edited by William A. Darity, Jr. (New York: MacMillan/Gale, 2007).

[45] Harry H. Laughlin, *Eugenical sterilization in the United States* (Chicago: Psychopathic Laboratory of the Municipal Court of Chicago, 1922).

[46] See 274 in the U.S. Supreme Court Center at www.justia.com.

[47] See 1924 VA, Acts 569.

prevent those who are manifestly unfit for continuing their kind. . . . Three generations is enough'.[48]

Although the case was later found to be based on fraudulent evidence, there were more than 65,000 such surgeries in the United States from 1907 until at least 1979. The threat of eugenic ideology was evident in different states, providing numerous interpretations for sterilisation. Most of those chosen by the states for sterilisation were poor and living in state institutions, proving that there was an economic reason for the mass sterilisations.

The Nazis partially based their eugenics programme on the programmes of forced sterilisation found in the United States. The Law for the Prevention of Hereditarily Diseased Offspring, the 'Sterilization Law', proclaimed on 14 July 1933, required physicians to register every case of hereditary illness known to them, except in women over forty-five years of age. Physicians could be fined for failing to comply. In 1934, the first year of the law's operation, nearly 4,000 people appealed against the decisions of sterilisation authorities; 3,559 of the appeals failed. By the end of the Nazi regime, more than 200 Hereditary Health Courts (*Erbgesundheitsgerichten*) were created, and under their rulings more than 400,000 people were sterilised against their will.[49]

The transition from sterilisation to euthanasia and the killing of children and adults born with physical deformities, intellectual disabilities or suffering from mental illness was a natural one for Adolf Hitler in order to maintain his eugenics ideology. He initiated the T4 programme named after the office located in Tiergartenstrasse 4 in Berlin, the headquarters of the euphemistically named Charitable Foundation for Curative and Institutional Care. Hitler placed the operation under the control of Philipp Bouhler, chief of the state chancellery, and Karl Brandt, Hitler's private physician. 'Defective' children were removed from their families and taken to 'hospitals', such as the Hartheim and Hadamar, 'euthanasia' killing centres where the exterminations were carried out. The programme was expanded to include adults to prevent any 'deficient' member of the

---

[48] *Buck v. Bell*, 274 U.S. 200 (1927).

[49] Robert J. Lifton, *The Nazi doctors: Medical killing and the psychology of genocide* (New York: Basic Books, 1986), pp. 22–144.

German 'master race' from breeding so they could not pass on their 'inferiority'.

One of the most important and well-known books about the Nazi euthanasia action was written by Ernst Klee: *'Euthanasie' im NS-Staat: Die 'Vernichtung lebensunwerten Lebens'*.[50] Klee describes the extermination 'hospitals' such as Grafeneck or Hartheim, where the first gas chambers were built before the Holocaust, and where mostly adult victims were suffocated with carbon monoxide. Klee describes further the killing of crippled children by doctors with lethal injections and the starvation of patients marked for extermination.

Klee also outlines the resistance from the churches and the relatives of the victims, which led to a slowdown in the killings and increased secrecy of the operation, but did not stop it. The operation was conducted still more covertly after August 1941, when seventy thousand people had already died in the gas chambers of Grafeneck, Hartheim, Hadamar, Bernburg, Brandenburg and Sonnenstein. By that time every third inmate of a psychiatric institution in Germany had already died, either by being actively killed or through starvation, leading to about ninety-three thousand 'free beds' – to use Nazi terminology – at the end of 1941.

TOWARD THE SECOND HALF OF THE TWENTIETH CENTURY AND THE BEGINNING OF THE TWENTY-FIRST CENTURY

In the second half of the twentieth century the United States witnessed significant changes in values and attitudes toward persons with disabilities.[51] The civil rights movement of the 1960s in the United States encouraged people with disabilities to become organised. In the early 1970s, they lobbied Congress to include civil rights language for people with disabilities in the 1972 Rehabilitation Act. The Act was vetoed by President Richard Nixon. After a group of people with disabilities marched on

---

[50] Ernst Klee (born in 1942 in Frankfurt am Main) is a German journalist and author. As a writer on Germany's history, he is best known for his exposure and documentation of the medical crimes of Adolf Hitler's Third Reich, much of which is concerned with the Action T4 forced euthanasia program.

[51] For a complete review, see Richard K. Scotch, 'American disability policy in the twentieth century'. In *The new disability history: American perspectives (History of disability)*. Edited by Paul K. Longmore and Lauri Umansky (New York: New York University Press, 2001).

Washington, a revised 1973 Rehabilitation Act was passed. Parallel to the disability rights movement, parents and advocates of children with disabilities struggled for access to educational services. The Individuals with Disabilities Education Act (IDEA) of 1990, called for a free and appropriate public education for every child with a disability to be delivered in the least restrictive and most integrated environment appropriate.[52]

Despite changes in rehabilitation and education law, people with disabilities did not achieve broad civil rights until the enactment of the Americans with Disabilities Act (ADA) in 1990.[53] This landmark federal antidiscrimination law ensured equal access to employment opportunities and public accommodations for people with disabilities. With this act, Congress identified the full participation, inclusion and integration of people with disabilities into society as a national goal.

Does the ADA reflect the positive change in the status of people with disabilities in the United States at the end of the twentieth century? Ruth Colker, who wrote the book *The Disability Pendulum: The First Decade of the Americans with Disabilities Act*, was critical of the role of the Supreme Court in the interpretation of the legislation.[54] She believed that the problem lay 'in the Rehnquist Court's twin decisions to invalidate parts of the ADA on constitutional law grounds (*Garret*), while also interpreting the statute narrowly in an entirely historical framework (*Sutton*)'.[55]

Similar developments were recorded in late twentieth and early twenty-first centuries. Countries such as the UK, Australia, Canada and Israel passed laws aimed at reducing discrimination against people with disabilities. These civil rights became the milestones for a global antidiscrimination and equal opportunity legislation. However, there was a significant gap between the innovative legislation and the current values, environmental barriers and social welfare policies. There is no doubt that the most remarkable international development was the United Nations Convention on the Rights of Persons with Disabilities (UN CRPD),[56] which

---

[52] Individuals with Disabilities Education Act 20 U.S.C. §§ 1400 et seq.

[53] Americans with Disabilities Act of 1990 (ADA) 42 U.S.C. §§ 12101 et seq.

[54] Ruth Colker, *The disability pendulum: The first decade of the Americans with Disabilities Act*. (New York: New York University Press, 2005).

[55] Ibid., p. 201.

[56] See the official website of the UN Convention on the Rights of Persons with Disabilities, www.un.org/disabilities/convention.

acknowledges equality, dignity, autonomy, independence, accessibility and inclusion as the keys to ensuring that people with disabilities are able to fully realise equal citizenship in the world. The convention came into force on 3 May 2008 and articulates a bold human rights framework for removing the barriers facing people with disabilities around the world. As the first convention of the twenty-first century, it is quickly becoming one of the most ratified treaties in the human rights system.

The twentieth century saw dramatic change with respect to the status of people with disabilities. At the beginning of the century, people with disabilities experienced exclusion, segregation and sterilisation. Many were marginalised and placed in large and inhuman institutions. At the end of the twentieth century, society had recognised their personal and social rights by responding with innovative domestic legislation and an international declaration ensuring their equality and dignity.

CONCEPTUALISATION OF DISABILITY

The conceptualisation of disability grew from victimisation and marginalisation in ancient times to inclusion and recognition of rights in our times. The past reflects the changes in societal perception of disability and in particular the roles that religion, values, culture and the legal and economic infrastructures played in defining disability. For example, Ancient Greece taught us that the economy played an important role in making the distinction between people with disabilities who could be self-sufficient and live and those who would be eliminated. In this context, pre-industrial and feudal times were agricultural and could accommodate people with disabilities.[57] Industrialisation marginalised people with physical disabilities because they could not fit into the regulated factory production system.

Despite the progress that has been recorded in the status of people with disabilities throughout history, there are current stereotypes that still exist today. Those in the media portraying people with disabilities as demonic or supernatural are rooted in the Middle Ages in Europe and

---

[57] For sociopolitical perspective, see Vic Finkelstein, *Attitudes and disabled people: Issues for discussion* (New York: World Rehabilitation Fund, 1980).

express how deep and ambivalent are our attitudes toward people with disabilities. Eugenics is still quite common in our society regardless of the dark impact and connotations it had in the twentieth century. In fact, there is debate in Western society about the merit of the 'new eugenics', and the promotion of genetic technologies to prevent the birth of babies with defects. It is perceived as progressive, sending a clear message that society has the power to do almost anything to eliminate the occurrence of disability. Preventing the breeding of the unfit has social consequences, as those who are born with a disability are perceived as failures and a social problem.[58]

There is a tendency in disability studies to blame the medical model for personalising disability and identifying people with disabilities according to their deficiency.[59] The explanation is simple: Medicalisation looks mainly for the deficit and has unintentionally created an inferior role for persons with a disability in our society. People with disabilities are judged by and compensated for their deficit, their inability to live independently and their dependency. The next section provides an interpretation of the changes that have been associated with moral, medical and social pathology models. The models have been transformed from an individualistic perspective focusing mainly on disablement to enablement, social functional models and rights approaches.[60]

CONCEPTUALISING DISABILITY: FROM DISABLEMENT TO ENABLEMENT

The conceptualisation of disability has run parallel to the historical societal perception of disability. The period before the twentieth century was associated with moral and religious views. The twentieth century departed from these traditional approaches by adopting new ideas. However, there are still traces of the earlier conceptualisations associating disability with pathology and mercy. Toward the end of the second half of the

---

[58] Stephen Garton, *Out of luck: Poor Australians and social welfare, 1788–1988* (Sydney: Allen & Unwin, 1990), pp. 43–61.

[59] Paul Longmore, 'Making disability an essential part of American history', *OAH Magazine of History*, 23 (2009), 11–15.

[60] Carmelo Masala and Donatella Rita Petretto, 'From disablement to enablement: Conceptual models of disability in the 20th century', *Disability and Rehabilitation* 30 (2008), 1233–44.

twentieth century, there was a significant shift toward a socio-functional approach, emphasising the role of the physical and social environment in conceptualising disability.

THE MORAL/RELIGIOUS MODEL

The moral or religious view of disability is historically the early perception of disability.[61] The Judeo-Christians perceived disability as an act of God and a sin or punishment inflicted upon an individual or family by an external, usually supernatural force. Birth conditions were associated with actions committed in a previous reincarnation. There was a link between a sin or immoral behaviour and the cause of psychosis or another mental illness. Therefore, the latter could be cured by acts of exorcism or sacrifice, or by justifying the persecution or even the death of the sinner. In some cases, the curse of negative expression of evil might stigmatise the whole family and exclude all members from social and civic participation. There were rare cases in which the family was viewed as a victim and as an object of spiritual compensation. The moral/religious model viewed disability as a personal tragedy.[62] Human beings could not fully understand the reason for suffering or choosing certain persons, but took comfort in recognising that it was God's will.

Although the model is outdated and less acceptable today, it is still prevalent today in Western societies.[63] One of the popular expressions used by psychotherapists is, 'God would not give you this cross to bear unless you could handle it'. A confirmation of this belief was found in a study of counsellors' attitudes toward people with disabilities, which revealed that most of them (75 percent), viewed disability as a personal tragedy.[64]

---

[61] See Jayne Clapton and Jennifer Fitzgerald, 'The history of disability: A history of otherness', *New Renaissance Magazine* 7 (1997). Available at http://www.ru.org/human-rights/the-history-of-disability-a-history-of-otherness.html.

[62] Michael Oliver, *Understanding disability: From theory to practice* (Basingstoke: Macmillan, 1996). Michael Oliver is Emeritus Professor of Disability Studies at the University of Greenwich and a disability rights activist. Much of his work has centered on advocating the social model of disability.

[63] For further reading, see Tobin Siebers, *Disability theory* (Ann Arbor: University of Michigan Press, 2008).

[64] Kaley Maureen Roosen, 'From tragedy to "crip" to human: The need for multiple understanding of disability in psychotherapy', *Critical Disability Discourse* 1 (2009), 1–27.

It is clear that the attitudes of such professionals toward disability shifts attention to the identified patient as being in need of pity and special care. Interestingly, these feelings of being chosen by God are often expressed by people with disabilities themselves.[65] A recent report on women with multiple sclerosis (MS) presented their justification for being sick as having been chosen by God to cope with the challenge of the MS.

THE MEDICAL MODEL

The medical model of disability emerged toward the middle of the eighteenth century. The basic assumption of the medical model is that disability is based on certain impairments. Francis Galton conceptualises disability, trying to link it to the conditions and length of illness and impairment of functional outcomes.[66] In the early 1950s, the common interpretation of disability was the identification of a pathology or impairment. Therefore, the primary role of the physician was to assess and determine the medical deficit associated with the impairment (or impairments). The first disability model that departed from classical medical thinking was offered by Nagi.[67]

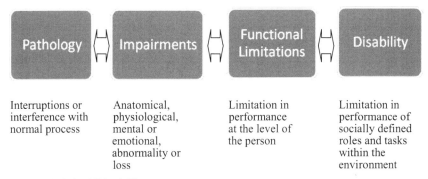

Pathology	Impairments	Functional Limitations	Disability
Interruptions or interference with normal process	Anatomical, physiological, mental or emotional, abnormality or loss	Limitation in performance at the level of the person	Limitation in performance of socially defined roles and tasks within the environment

Nagi Model of Disability

[65] Kenneth I. Pakenham, 'Making sense of illness or disability', *Journal of Health Psychology* 13 (2008), 99.

[66] See Oliver, *Understanding disability*.

[67] Adapted from Saad Z. Nagi, 'Some conceptual issues in disability and rehabilitation'. In *Sociology and rehabilitation*. Edited by Marvin B. Sussman (Washington, D.C.: American Sociological Association, 1965), pp. 100–13.

Nagi was the first scholar who disagreed with the assumption that the presence of impairment was enough to determine disability. He renamed the process whereby the person with a given disability has some functional limitations and some disabilities 'disablement' to highlight its dynamic nature.[68] According to Nagi, disability is an 'expression of a physical or a mental limitation in a social context, a gap between the individual's capabilities and the demands created by the physical and the social environment'. The model was revised and is well known as the IOM (Institute of Medicine) model of disability and contributed to the definition of criteria of eligibility in Social Security Insurance and Supplemental Security Income in the United States.

The second contribution to the development of the medical model was the epidemiological survey of impairment and handicapped people in Great Britain carried out by Amelia I. Harris and the Office of Population Censuses and Surveys Social Survey Division.[69] Two central terms served as the indicators for disability: 'impairment' and 'handicap'. Impairment was defined as the loss of a limb, partially or wholly, or the presence of a dysfunctional limb, organ or body part. 'Handicap' was interpreted as loss or reduction of one or more functional abilities (mainly self-care).

The best-known medical model of disability was the International Classification of Impairments, Disabilities and Handicaps (ICIDH),[70] which is based on four principal events: (1) something abnormal occurs within an individual; (2) someone becomes aware of this occurrence; (3) the performance or behaviour of the individual may be altered as a result; and (4) the awareness itself, or the altered performance or behaviour to which this gives rise, may place this person at a disadvantage relative to others. This succession of events, from an interiorised to an

---

[68] Masala and Petretto, 'From disablement to enablement', 1233–4.

[69] Amelia I. Harris, with Elizabeth Cox and Christopher R. V. Smith, *Handicapped and impaired in Great Britain: Income and entitlement to supplementary benefit of impaired people* (London: HMSO, 1971).

[70] In 1980, the World Health Organization (WHO) published a tool for the classification of the consequences of disease, the International Classification of Impairments, Disabilities and Handicaps (ICIDH). It was field-tested in several countries and a revision process was begun in 1995 to address, inter alia, the need to use the classification as a framework for reporting of the health status of populations.

exteriorised experience, culminates in a socialisation of the experience which has three dimensions represented in the scheme below[71]:

Disease $\implies$ **Impairment** $\implies$ **Disability** $\implies$ **Handicap**
or Disorder

functional/loss   activity/limitation   social disadvantage

organ level   *person level*   *societal level*

The International Classification of Impairments, Disabilities and Handicaps (ICIDH) Model

The three terms are defined as follows: (1) *impairment* – any loss or abnormality of psychological, physiological or anatomical structure or function; (2) *disability* – any restriction or lack (resulting from impairment) of ability to perform an activity in the manner or within the range considered normal for human being; and (3) *handicap* – a disadvantage for a given individual, resulting from an impairment or a disability, that limits or prevents the fulfilment of a role that is normal (depending on age, gender and social and cultural factors) for that individual.

Interestingly, the model proposes multiple links among the three levels instead of linear connection. As it offers integration between medical components and the consequences of disease, it therefore provides a common international terminology for all, applicable to individual assessment as well as to surveys and research.[72]

The main criticism against the ICIDH is that it focuses on the individual and on his/her personal experience. The physical and social environments are interpreted through personal eyes. In addition, the model has been attacked by leaders of the United States and British disability movements (such as the Society for Disability Studies, Disabled People International and others) as focusing primarily on a person's deficit, without considering the important roles of the environmental and social barriers.[73]

---

[71] Adapted from the ICIDH (Geneva: WHO, 1980).

[72] Mary Chamie, 'Survey design strategy for the study of disability', *World Health Statistics Quarterly* 42 (1989), 122–40.

[73] Masala and Petretto, 'From disablement to enablement', 1233–44.

It should be noted that Nagi himself revised his model to add the social perspective by stating that disability refers to 'social rather than organismic functioning'.[74] In this sense, Nagi's interpretation of environment was taken from the viewpoint of the demands posed to the individual, while the disablement process was perceived as a function of the nature of the impairment as related to the functional limitation.

An interesting effort to revise the Nagi and the ICIDH models was carried out by the National Center for Medical Rehabilitation Research (NCMRR) at Bethesda, Maryland. The new model defined disability as 'a limitation in performing tasks, activities, and roles to levels expected within physical and social contexts'.[75] Finally, additional revisions that viewed the disablement as a consequence of the interaction between the individual and the environment add some clarification to the model.[76] Clearly, the effort showed that the medical model has gone a long way from defining disability as a core expression of pathology and impairment to an interactive one between the individual with an impairment and the environment. With respect to social inclusion, the medical model is based on a deficit and therefore has been less sensitive to stereotypes of disability that are associated with the pathology. Furthermore, the model's individual orientation imposes on the person with the disability the main responsibility for his/her mainstreaming and integration into society.

THE SOCIAL MODEL

The social model arose in response to the shortcomings of the medical model of disability. One of the most significant critiques was written by Mike Oliver, who thought that disability 'as a category can only be understood within the framework which suggests that it is culturally produced

---

[74] Saad Z. Nagi, 'Disability concepts revisited: Implications for prevention'. In *Disability in America: Toward a national agenda for prevention*. Edited by Andrew M. Pope and Alvin R. Tarlov (Washington D.C.: National Academy Press, 1991), p. 309.

[75] National Centre for Medical Rehabilitation Research (NCMRR), 'Research plan for the National Centre for Medical Rehabilitation Research', National Institute of Child Health & Human Development of the National Institutes of Health. Public Health Service: NIH Publication No. 93-3509, 1993, p. 24.

[76] See Edward N. Brandt and Andrew M. Pope, *Enabling America: Assessing the role of rehabilitation science and engineering* (Washington D.C.: National Academy Press, 1997).

and socially structured'.[77] The social model was based on the struggle of two important movements: the Independent Living Movement and the Disability Rights Movement in the United States. However, from a sociopolitical standpoint, the social model has been viewed as a Minority Group Model of Disability, keeping society responsible for denying the needs and aspirations of people with disabilities.

Conceptually, the social model is associated with the revision of the International Classification of Functioning, Disability and Health (ICF), which drew on experience with other disability models, most notably Nagi's conceptualisation. The ICF comprises a biopsychosocial model in which a person's functioning and disability is conceived of as a dynamic interaction between health conditions and both environmental and personal contextual factors.[78]

INTERNATIONAL CLASSIFICATION OF FUNCTIONING (ICF)

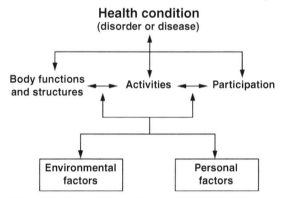

International Classification of Functioning (ICF) Model

The ICF[79] identifies three levels of human function[80]: functioning at the level of body or body parts, the whole person and the whole person in their complete environment. These levels, in turn, contain three domains of human function: body functions and structures, activities and

---

[77] Mike Oliver, *The politics of disablement* (London: MacMillan, 1990), p. 22.

[78] International Classification of Functioning, Disability and Health (ICF), www.who.int/entity/classifications/icf/en/.

[79] Adapted from the ICF (Geneva: WHO, 2001).

[80] Alan M. Jette, 'Toward a common language for function, disability, and health', *Physical Therapy* 86 (2006), 726–34.

participation. The term *disability* is used to denote a decrement at each level, impairment, an activity limitation and a participation restriction.

The first domain of the ICF model is *body functions and structures*, which are defined in the context of health experience – *body functions* are the physiological functions of body systems (including psychological functions), while *body structures* are anatomical parts of the body such as organs, limbs and their components. *Impairments* are problems in body function or structure as a significant deviation or loss. Impairments within the ICF include deviations from generally accepted population standards in the biomedical status of the body and its function and can be temporary or permanent.

The model defines the *activity* and *participation* domains in the context of health experience: *Activity* is the execution of a task or action by an individual; *activity limitations* are defined as difficulties an individual may have in executing activities. *Participation* is involvement in a life situation, while *participation restrictions* are problems an individual may experience in involvement in life situations.

The ICF can be applied at the individual, institutional and social levels. At the individual level, it is used for the assessment of an individual's level of functioning, treatment planning and maximisation of intervention. At the institutional level, the ICF can be used for education and training, planning and development and as a management and outcome evaluation instrument. Finally, at the social level, the ICF is expected to be used for eligibility criteria for state entitlements such as social security benefits, disability pensions, workers' compensation and insurance, social policy development, including legislative reviews, model legislation, regulations and guidelines, and definitions for antidiscrimination legislation and for needs assessment.

However, the social model has been criticised by specialists for minimising the importance of the medical perspective of disability and, in particular, the importance of the emotional and bodily experiences of people with disabilities. In addition, there is a concern about the clash between the social model and social welfare legislation and entitlements.[81] The concern is one of impracticality as the current qualifying standards

[81] Masala and Petretto, 'From disablement to enablement', 1242–4.

for benefits are primarily medical. It is unclear how these extreme mani-
festations can be bridged.

RELIGION, HISTORY, CONCEPTUALISATION AND SOCIAL INCLUSION OF PEOPLE WITH DISABILITIES

The Bible reflects a dualistic approach to disability that ranges from
mercy to segregation, supernatural image and marginalisation. Disability
is expressed as God's will, as a sin, as a punishment or as a revers-
ible impairment that can be healed. The Qur'an does not differentiate
disability from other conditions of disadvantage. Ancient Greece and
Rome teach us about early eugenics, infanticide and the roots of negative stereotypes associated with disabilities. Greece and Rome set the
stage for a pragmatic definition of disability that has been associated
with self-sufficiency and early guardianship legislation. The Middle Ages
and early modern periods intensified the negative images attached to
disability, with witchcraft and the marginalisation of people with disabilities setting the background for segregation. However, the early modern
period again raised the need for eugenics legislation and regulating practices and medicalisation approaches to disability. The primary approach
was the medical model associated with social welfare policies. Most of
the countries in the twentieth century depended heavily on social welfare policies and means and tested legislation and programmes that the
disability movement had targeted as obstacles to social equality.[82]

The medical model is based on the development of scientific knowledge: The doctor replaced the priest and the rabbi as a social agent in
shaping values and curing processes. The model can be regarded as an
individual model, where disability is conceived of as part of the disease
process, as an abnormality and as an individual tragedy. This approach
emphasises the deficit and implies that only those who are considered
'incapable' or 'unproductive' are entitled to certain benefits. In return,
they are viewed by society as officially exempted and excluded from the
mainstream.

---

[82] Graham Room, *Beyond the threshold: The measurement and analysis of social exclusion* (Bristol:
The Policy Press, 1995).

The social model, associated also with a rights-based model of disability, offers a departure from the deficit and tragedy approaches. This sociopolitical construct emphasises the shift from dependence to independence, as people with disabilities have been given the right to seek a civic and political voice. The social model is interpreted as the 'barriers approach', where disability is referred to environmental, structural and attitudinal barriers that impinge upon the lives of people with disabilities. These barriers include inaccessible education or lack of education, inaccessible information and communication systems, inaccessible working environments, inadequate or lacking disability benefits, discriminatory health and social-care services, and inaccessible transport, housing, public buildings and amenities.

Finally, the social model of disability also introduces negative societal attitudes and stereotypes that preclude people with disabilities from social inclusion. Therefore, it is not clear whether the conceptual change reduces social exclusion and enhances their integration into society. A thorough review of social exclusion and social inclusion conceptualisation may provide better insights about the status of people with disabilities nationally and internationally.

3   SOCIAL EXCLUSION AND SOCIAL INCLUSION

CONCEPTUALISING SOCIAL EXCLUSION/SOCIAL INCLUSION

The history of disability demonstrates that people with disabilities lived on the margin of society, excluded from opportunities (e.g., housing, employment, healthcare, civic engagement, democratic participation and due process) and human rights. This chapter introduces the concept of social exclusion and its relationship to social inclusion. In addition, it provides expressions of social exclusion and inclusion among people with disabilities, as well as ways of measuring and analysing them.

DEFINITIONS AND ROOTS

Social exclusion is a complex concept that expresses disadvantages in relation to certain norms of social, economic or political activity related to individuals, households, spatial areas or population group. The term is inclusive and is used to describe a process through which disadvantage comes about and also to present the outcomes or consequences for individuals, groups or communities. Its roots appeared in Durkheim's classical social theory to reflect the transition from agrarian to industrial society in European society.[1] It is often mentioned as a substitute for terms such as disadvantage, injustice, discrimination and poverty, and particularly state of poverty. It is an opposite term to social

---

[1] See, for example, Steven Lukes, *Emile Durkheim: His life and work: A historical and critical study* (Palo Alto, CA: Stanford University Press, 1985).

inclusion, and sometimes refers to poor urban housing. Although social scientists consider it to be multidimensional, there is disagreement as to which dimensions are more important or dominant. Social exclusion may overlap not only with poverty, employment and economic distress but also with terms such as social capital and social participation.

In terms of policy, social exclusion is a European concept that originated in France in the mid-1970s. It was used by French socialist governments to describe the margins of society; that is, people who lack access to the social insurance system. The invention of the term social exclusion is usually attributed to René Lenoir, then Secrétaire d'Etat a l'Action Sociale in the Chirac government, who published *Les Exclus: Un Français sur dix* in 1974.[2] Lenoir's exclusion included a wide variety of people, not only the poor but also the suicidal, the aged, people with disabilities, abused children and substance abusers – about 10 percent of the French population.

Social exclusion was adopted by the European Union (EU) in the late 1980s as a key concept to describe its antipoverty policy.[3] The effort was to combat stigma attached to 'poverty' and 'deprivation'. However, the meaning transformed from poverty to marginalisation and unemployment. Interestingly, social exclusion was widely used in France and the UK but hardly in the United States. In France, the term expanded to encompass more groups of people on the margins of society, and came to denote a 'rupture of the social bond', expressing the desired contract between the state and its citizens.[4] In the UK, the concept reflected the relative deprivation of poverty.[5] The concept went beyond material deprivation and was interpreted with respect to restricted opportunities to participate in wider social and cultural activities. In the United States,

---

[2] See René Lenoir, *Les exclus: Un Français sur dix* (Paris: Le Seuil, 1974).

[3] Rob Atkinson and Simin Davoudi, 'The concept of social exclusion in the European Union: Context, development and possibilities', *Journal of Common Market Studies* 38 (2000), 427–48.

[4] Hilary Silver and S. M. Miller, 'Social exclusion: The European approach to social disadvantage', *Indicators* 2 (2003), 5–21.

[5] See definition by Angus Cameron, 'Progress on welfare and exclusion II: Social inclusion and exception', *Progress in Human Geography* 30 (2006), 396–404.

it was consonant with terms such as 'underclass', 'disadvantage' and 'welfare dependency'.

SOCIAL INCLUSION

Social inclusion and social exclusion are often viewed as inseparable sides of the same coin. *Inclusion* is viewed as a desirable outcome or as a strategy to combat social exclusion, whereas *exclusion* is viewed as an expression of poor social cohesion. Surprisingly, there is limited literature about social inclusion, a term which has not been defined in its own right. It is defined exclusively as a desired goal that requires equality of opportunity and participation in the rudimentary and fundamental functions of society.[6] However, this definition has been criticised for being inadequate because it is often used as a desired goal or with respect to problems and deficits. Social inclusion is therefore most commonly defined as being the opposite of social exclusion. For this reason, much of the discussion of the measurement of social inclusion is dominated by a simplistic exclusion-social exclusion formulation.

Dunn made a descriptive distinction between the two terms by claiming that 'Social inclusion must come down to somewhere to live, something to do, someone to love'.[7] Social exclusion has been interpreted as a 'compound process' that operates in all areas of life – daily living, work and training, and access to services including health, insurance, consumer and leisure services.[8] However, there are cases where there can be simultaneous exclusion and inclusion. People or groups can be excluded in one domain and included in another. For example, immigrants or people with disabilities can have respected and dignified lives within their extended families but at the same time experience rejection and denial of their rights within their communities.

---

[6] See Julie Repper and Rachel Perkins, *Social inclusion and recovery: A model for mental health practice* (London: Elsevier Health Sciences, 2003).

[7] Sara Dunn, *Creating accepting communities: Report of the MIND inquiry into social exclusion and mental health problems* (London: Mind, 1999), viii.

[8] Ibid., pp. ix and 6.

PARADIGMS

There are two core conceptualisations of social exclusion in the European literature.[9,10] Silver based his paradigm on European and political thought and Levitas on Blair's New Labour social policy. Silver offered three paradigms of social exclusion: (1) the solidarity paradigm, which is rooted in the French ideas of social solidarity; (2) the specialisation paradigm, which is prevalent in the United States and the UK and is often associated with discrimination; and (3) the monopoly paradigm, which is commonly used in Western Europe to strengthen group monopoly. Solidarity refers to social relations and the effort to create a cohesive society. In this case, social exclusion is perceived as a lack of solidarity or crisis in shared values and rights. Specialisation is consonant with pluralism and public choice; therefore, exclusion occurs when there are core barriers to the flow of exchanges between individuals or among groups. Monopoly is usually associated with Marxism and social exclusion with oppression of the needy or poor.

DIMENSIONS OF SOCIAL EXCLUSION

Percy-Smith views social exclusion as a central concern for social policy in the European Union and the United States.[11] Although the term is amorphous and used to describe a process or outcome, it is perceived as multidimensional. It may relate to economic, political and spatial exclusion, as well as lack of access to specific areas such as information, medical provision, housing, policing and security. These dimensions are seen to be interrelated and reinforce each other and as being associated with participation in full citizenship.

In 1999 the Department of Social Security in the UK listed the following modes of social exclusion: lack of opportunities to work; lack of opportunities to acquire education and skills; childhood deprivation;

---

[9] See Hilary Silver, 'Social exclusion and social solidarity: Three paradigms', *International Labor Review* 133 (1994), 531–77.

[10] Ruth Levitas, *The inclusive society? Social exclusion and the new labor* (London: Macmillan, 1998).

[11] For extensive review see Janie Percy-Smith, 'The contours of social exclusion'. In *Policy responses to social exclusion.* Edited by J. Percy-Smith (Buckingham: Open University Press, 2000).

disrupted families; barriers to older people living active and healthy lives; inequalities in health; poor housing; poor neighbourhoods; fear of crime; and disadvantaged groups.[12] The checklist includes diversified items that lack common conceptualisation.

A more conceptual framework of social exclusion, with five dimensions, was offered by Burchardt et al.[13] Social exclusion has been interpreted in terms of social and civic participation and has included consumption, saving, production, political and social activity. An individual's ability to participate in these activities will be affected by a range of interconnected factors including personal experience and life history, the characteristics of the area in which they live and the social, civil and political institutions with which they have to interact. It is interesting that this conceptualisation has been adopted in the disability area, more than those that were linked with poverty and economic indicators.

It is clear that social exclusion cannot be conceptualised separately from economic, social, political, neighbourhood and spatial, individual and group factors. The economic factor is defined in terms of lack of an adequate income and unemployment, in addition to macro changes in the economy and labour market. The social aspect is defined as a breakdown of social norms and is expressed in deviance and crime. The political dimension is reflected in the ability of people to participate in or make decisions that affect their lives. The neighbourhood and spatial dimension of social exclusion presents the inability of local support networks to provide decent housing and services associated with combating neglect and decaying conditions. All aspects of social exclusion have an impact on the individual that are clearly expressed by poor health (physical and mental), education and career development (underachievement) indicators and low self-esteem. Finally, the group dimension of social exclusion is reflected in being different in some way from the dominant population or being marginalised in terms of social status.

An interesting interpretation of social exclusion was offered by Berman and Philips.[14] They proposed three distinctions between *demos*

---

[12] Department of Social Security, *Opportunity for all tackling poverty and social exclusion* (London: First Annual Report, HMSO Cm 4445, 1999).

[13] Tania Burchardt, Julian Le Grand and David Plachaud, 'Social exclusion in Britain 1991–1995', *Social Policy and Administration* 33 (1999), 227–44.

[14] For an extensive review see James S. Coleman, *Foundations of social theory* (Cambridge, MA: Harvard University Press, 1990).

and *ethnos*. Demos reflects social exclusion at the national level, while ethnos expresses exclusion that is evident within the community. Social exclusion at the national level (demos) means that governments cannot offer accessible rights to their citizens. Social exclusion at the community level (ethnos) is basically a micro-psychological approach that expresses the degree of participation or acceptance in day-to-day life.

THE INTERRELATIONS BETWEEN SOCIAL INCLUSION/SOCIAL EXCLUSION AND SOCIAL CAPITAL

The term *social capital* is widely used in the areas of health, education and community programmes. For example, the World Bank uses social capital as a means to the end of economic growth, the necessary social glue that allows unfettered markets to work the magic of their invisible hands. Policy makers and community planners tend to define social capital as a network of social relationships that help people to get along with each other and act more effectively than they could as individuals. The term is consonant with human trust, mutuality and reciprocity and acting so that people can benefit as individuals, groups and members in society.

There are two common approaches to social capital. The first was defined by Coleman as a resource that accrues to individuals by virtue of their access to contacts, connections and linkages. It recognises the importance of networking as a viable asset. Clearly, people who can expand their networking and use it effectively are considered as having social capital.[15] The latter is defined as an aggregate of the actual or potential resources that are linked to possession of a durable network of more or less institutionalised relationships of mutual acquaintance and recognition. It may exist only in the practical state (i.e., in material and/or symbolic exchanges, which help to maintain them). They may also be socially instituted and guaranteed through the application of a family, a class, a school or a party. There is no doubt that educated people who can access information are considered to be resourceful.

---

[15] For a broader review, see Pierre Bourdieu, 'The forms of capital'. In *Handbook of theory and research for the sociology of education*. Edited by John G. Richardson (New York: Greenwood, 1986), pp. 241–258.

The second approach is that social capital is the property of groups and those who work through the mode of institutional economics,[16] and is basically attained by mutual learning and how well they can work together. The main beneficiary of social capital is therefore the public at large. While it may benefit individuals and the groups to which people belong, the main effect of social capital is on society at large by changing the institutional basis for interpersonal relationships. Social capital and social inclusion/social exclusion are significant concepts in human services but their interrelationship remains largely unexplored. They may overlap or be used interchangeably to refer to the interface between economical assets and society. Daly and Silver offered an interesting table to demonstrate the interrelation between the two concepts.[17]

Comparative View of Social Exclusion and Social Capital

Focus	Social exclusion	Social capital
Dominant orientation	The 'social problem'	Social progress
Theoretical reference	French Republicanism, social democracy	Communitarians, social exchange, rational choice
Regional application	Europe, Latin America	United States, developing countries
Purpose of concept	To frame or reframe social problems and promote welfare	To instrumentalise social relations for economic growth and democratic functioning
Desired outcome	Include individuals, cohesive societies	Collective action, economic growth, democratic functioning
Empirical operationalisation	Persistent poverty, long-term unemployment, degree of involvement in social relations	Quantity of memberships, amount of trust or corruption

---

[16] Elinor Ostrom, 'Social capital: A fad or fundamental concept?' In *Social capital: A multifaceted perspective*. Edited by Partha Dasgupta and Ismail Serageldin (Washington, D.C.: The World Bank, 1999), pp. 172–214.

[17] Adapted from Mary Daly and Hilary Silver, 'Social exclusion and social capital: A comparison and critique', *Theory and Society* 37 (2008), 540.

It is clear that the two concepts overlap with respect to their focus as both are geared toward engagement, participation and connectedness and to some degree in their desired outcome. Both strive to enhance cohesiveness and the collective action of people, groups and organisations. However, the two concepts differ in their orientation and purpose. Social exclusion is expressed as a social problem and a search for solutions, whereas social capital is a tool aimed at promoting growth.

In terms of usage and implications, social exclusion and social capital are frequently used in international and domestic policy, primarily with respect to poverty, employment and housing. The concepts are often used as ways to deal with high unemployment in Europe and governmental failure to offer a conventional solution to this problem. However, there is criticism of its connection to social exclusion/social inclusion. People who are considered socially excluded do not always lack social capital, as the lack of social inclusion is not always attributed to society's failure to regulate it.[18] For example, people with vision impairment often think that they have fairly good social capital and networking, but they are still excluded by employers due to stigma.

SOCIAL EXCLUSION AND STIGMA

The experience of being excluded is often associated with negative emotions and feelings and a sense of sadness, loneliness, anger, shame and anxiety.[19] It can be expressed by episodic *interpersonal rejection* or *peer rejection*. Although most of us experience some level of rejection in our lives, rejection can become a problem when it is prolonged or consistent, when the relationship is important or when an individual is highly concerned about being rejected. Rejection of an entire group of people, such as people with disabilities, can have negative effects, particularly when it results in social avoidance or isolation.

The process of exclusion is reflected by personal or intimate rejection, by distancing and by the development of stigmatisation and prejudiced

---

[18] Charles Kadushin, 'Too much investment in social capital?' *Social Networks* 26 (2004), 75–90.

[19] See Marc. R. Leary, *Interpersonal rejection* (New York: Oxford University Press, 2001).

attitudes toward members of stigmatised groups.[20] Exclusion is therefore basically a disassociation process that ends with stigmatisation, 'when a shared characteristic of a category of people becomes consensually regarded as a basis for dissociating from (that is, avoiding, excluding, ostracising, or otherwise minimising interaction with) individuals who are perceived to be members of that category'.[21]

Do stigmatised people always experience social exclusion? Some scholars believed that exclusion of those who are stigmatised boosts the self-esteem of the non-stigmatised.[22] The theory of downward comparison posits that persons experiencing negative effects can enhance their subjective well-being through comparison with a less fortunate other. There are different processes that can ignite such comparisons such as choosing certain people for social comparison, projection and social prejudice. There is no doubt that the justification is directly linked to structured social inequalities that are common in a particular society or culture.[23] These attitudes may explain social, economic and political discrimination toward minorities and marginalised groups.

It appears that the process of exclusion and stigmatisation is evolutionary in nature and represents the rejection of groups that appear to be a burden on society. Based on the interpretation above, it is clear why the eugenic movement in the United States and Europe has been associated with exclusion practice and stigmatisation toward people with disabilities who are perceived as 'genetically inferior'.

People who experienced stigma-based exclusion react in different ways. They can improve their social value to others, or look for other kinds of relationships that will boast their status. Conversely, they may withdraw from intimate and social contact in order to avoid frustration and rejection. Interestingly, Crocker and Major showed three modes of

---

[20] Cheryl R. Kaiser and Carol T. Miller, 'Reacting to impending discrimination: Compensation for prejudice and attributions to discrimination', *Personality and Social Psychology Bulletin* 27 (2001), 1357–67.

[21] Mark R. Leary and Lisa R. Screindorfer, 'The stigmatization of HIV and AIDS: Rubbing salt in the wound'. In *HIV infection and social interaction*. Edited by V. Derlega and A. Barbee (Thousand Oaks, CA: Sage Publications, 1998), p. 15.

[22] Thomas A. Wills, 'Downward comparison principles in social psychology', *Psychological Bulletin* 90 (1981), 245–71.

[23] See Dominic Abrams, Julie Christian and David Gordon, *Multidisciplinary handbook of social exclusion research* (Oxford: Wiley-Blackwell, 2007).

cognitive processes used by people who have been excluded or are under threat of being stigmatised. The first is sticking to their own vulnerable group where they can freely discuss their thoughts without being concerned about losing their sense of appreciation. The second is minimising the attributes in which their group fares poorly and valuing those in which their group does better. The third is a reverse mode; that is, turning the negative attitudes toward those who reject them.[24] However, these processes are not always effective in minimising their sense of lost self-esteem or the social cost attached to it.

MEASURING SOCIAL INCLUSION/EXCLUSION

Is social inclusion or social exclusion measureable? It is unclear whether it is measureable and based on hard data or whether it actually expresses disadvantage, discrimination or injustice.[25] The common approach is to adopt a relative measure, comparing the status of the excluded sub-population with the general public by using multiple indicators, usually preexisting data.

However, relative multiple outcomes are not enough to understand and monitor states of social exclusion. Therefore, it is necessary to understand and monitor the process of social exclusion and to identify the factors that can trigger entry or exit from situations of exclusion.[26] There is also a need to use qualitative approaches such as techniques developed by ethnographic, discourse and rhetoric research in order to get an in-depth understanding of what people are thinking about their deprived or positive social conditions. It is also important to examine the context and the objectives of the evaluation, which is aimed at supporting a corrective policy, or to obtain a subjective expression of the experience of people in their own culture.

---

[24] Jennifer Crocker and Brenda Major, 'Social stigma and self-esteem: The self-protective properties of stigma', *Psychological Review* 96 (1989), 608–30.

[25] Craig Morgan, et al., 'Social exclusion and mental health: Conceptual and methodological review', *The British Journal of Psychiatry* 191 (2007), 477–83.

[26] Robert Walker, 'The dynamics of poverty and social exclusion'. In *Beyond the threshold: The measurement and analysis of social exclusion.* Edited by Graham Room (Bristol: The Policy Press, 1997), pp. 102–28.

MEASURING SOCIAL INCLUSION/EXCLUSION
IN THE DISABILITY AREA

What are the measures of social exclusion in the disability area? Do researchers use the same indicators as in other states of social deprivation or subpopulations? According to Morgan et al.,[27] who reviewed eight studies on social exclusion in mental health, the most frequently used method is employing indicators across a number of domains or dimensions.[28]

There are also qualitative measures exploring the relationship between reported mental health problems and conditions of social exclusion.[29] Specifically, Parr et al. have suggested that there is a need to look beyond indicators to the 'experiential processes . . . leading particular individuals and groupings to be excluded from the norms of everyday social life, activity and participation'.[30]

INDICATORS OF SOCIAL INCLUSION/EXCLUSION
OF PEOPLE WITH DISABILITIES

Most of the studies on social inclusion/social exclusion used domestic and international indicators. The following sections will illustrate the merit of using such indicators. Three illustrations are included. The first is taken from the Kessler Foundation and National Organization on Disability (Kessler/NOD) Report of 2010, which provides a retrospective look at the changes that have occurred in the United States since the ADA;[31]

---

[27] Morgan et al., 'Social exclusion and mental health', 473–80.

[28] The references of studies quoted by Craig Morgan et al. are listed on pp. 470–80 (They are Bonner et al., 2002; Shimitras et al., 2003; Targosz et al., 2003; Hjern et al., 2004; Todd et al., 2004; Webber and Huxley, 2004; Fakhoury and Priebe, 2006; and Payne, 2006).

[29] See, for example, Sara Dunn, 'Creating accepting communities: Report of the Mind enquiry into social exclusion and mental health problems', *Mind* (1999); Hester Parr, Chris Philo and Nicola Burns, 'Social geographies of rural mental health: Experiencing inclusions and exclusions', *Transactions of the Institute of British Geographers* 29 (2004), 401–19.

[30] Parr et al., 'Social geographies of rural mental health', 47.

[31] Kessler Foundation, *The 2010 survey of Americans with disabilities*. Accessed 17 October 2011, http://www.2010DisabilitySurveys.org.

the second is the Leonard Cheshire Disability report of 2008 on Disability Poverty in the UK;[32] and the third is the 2003 cross-country study of social inclusion in Organisation for Economic Co-operation and Development (OECD) countries.[33]

SOCIAL INCLUSION/EXCLUSION OF PEOPLE WITH DISABILITIES IN THE UNITED STATES

The most comprehensive effort examining indicators of social inclusion among people with disabilities in the United States was carried out by Kessler/NOD. These organisations commissioned Harris Interactive to conduct a series of surveys comparing their status to those without disabilities using ten indicators such as employment, income, education, healthcare, access to transportation, socialising, dining out in restaurants, attendance at religious services, political participation and life satisfaction.[34] The primary purpose of the 2010 research was measuring the size of the gaps of these indicators between people with and without disabilities over a period of twenty-four years. Three indicators were added in 2010: access to mental health services, technology and overall financial situation.

Analysis of social inclusion indicators demonstrated that there was a modest improvement among a few indicators, while the general trend of the measures was that twenty years after the passage of the ADA there has yet to be significant progress in many areas. Since 1986, substantial improvement has been reported in education attainment and political participation. However, large gaps were observed in employment, household income, access to transportation, healthcare, socialising, dining out in restaurants and satisfaction with life. In some instances, the spread has actually worsened since the inception of the survey in 1986.

---

[32] Leonard Cheshire Disability, *Disability poverty in the UK* (2008), 1–72, Accessed 11 July 2010, http://www.lcdisability.org/?lid=6386.

[33] Organization for Economic Co-operation and Development (OECD), *Transforming disability into ability: Policies to promote work and income security for disabled people* (Paris: OECD Publishing, 2003).

[34] Kessler Foundation, *The 2010 survey of Americans with disabilities*, Accessed 16 November 2011, http://www.2010DisabilitySurveys.org.

Unfortunately, the largest gap was still observed in employment, demonstrating that the employment rate of people with disabilities has not changed much since the legislation of the ADA in 1990. Interestingly, there are two areas where the gap has decreased – satisfaction with life and transportation – and two additional indicators that demonstrated a decreased gap: education and political participation.

Most of the unemployed attributed their restricted patterns of participation to the lack of adequate financial resources, accessible transportation and encouragement from community organisations. The fact that the survey was conducted during a significant economic downturn might explain the low employment rate, poverty and reduction in consumption. Beyond that, findings indicate that employment and community participation patterns may reinforce each other and serve as useful vehicles for promoting social integration for people with disabilities in their communities.

The Kessler/NOD 2010 Survey of Americans with Disabilities demonstrated that there were some positive gains in income and social participation measures, which is evident also in their sense of inclusion: Around three-quarters (72 percent) stated that they were treated the same as others when people learned they had a disability. Unfortunately, people with more severe disabilities were much more likely to describe negative experiences when asked how people generally react toward them: About half reported negative experiences, compared to 29 percent with slight or moderate disabilities.

The most encouraging indicator was education, where there was a remarkable reduction in people with disabilities who had not completed high school. However, it is surprising that this improvement had not translated into significant changes in employment rates. A possible explanation is that there is a lag of ten to fifteen years in translating these gains into higher employment rates.

DISABILITY AND POVERTY IN THE UK

A common expression of social exclusion is poverty or social deprivation. A recent UK report published by Leonard Cheshire Disability provides a unique opportunity to examine social exclusion based on indicators.[35] The report, which traces disability poverty in the UK, looks not only at financial poverty but also poverty of opportunity and the emotional poverty of people with disabilities.

Overall, people with disabilities in the UK are twice as likely to live in poverty as those without disabilities. Based on the 'relative poverty line' in the UK, which equates to living in a household with an income of less than 60 percent of median national income,[36] recent estimates suggest that around 30 percent of people with disabilities live below this income line compared to around 16 percent of non-disabled people. Compared to people without disabilities, those with disabilities have additional costs associated with the impact of their disability or illness. When the extra costs are factored in, more than half of the people with disabilities live on less than 60 percent of median national income as opposed to the unadjusted figure of 30 percent.[37] It is therefore clear that it is impossible to save money and be prepared for retirement.[38]

DISABILITY AND EMPLOYMENT

About half of the people with disabilities do not work compared to 20 percent of people without disabilities.[39] Unfortunately, even people with disabilities who are employed have significantly lower incomes than their non-disabled peers. In addition, they are more likely to work in lower-skilled and low-paying jobs.

DISABILITY AND HOUSING

A recent survey on quality of accommodation for people with disabilities showed a shortage of affordable and accessible housing for those who

---

[35] Leonard Cheshire Disability, *Disability poverty in the UK*, 1–72.
[36] Ibid., 15–23.
[37] Ibid., 21–3.
[38] Ibid., 41–3.
[39] Office of National Statistics, Labor Force Survey, 2007. Accessed 16 November 2011, http://www.nso.gov.mt/statdoc/document_view.aspx?id=2315&backUrl=publication_catalogue.aspx.

need it. A quarter of those who require adapted housing in England are currently living in accommodation that is unsuitable for their needs.[40]

DISABILITY AND EDUCATION

The UK Labour Force Survey of 2007 showed that about a 25 percent of people with disabilities at working age had no qualifications compared to 11 percent of non-disabled people. Young people with disabilities were twice as likely not to be in any form of education, employment or training as their non-disabled peers (15 percent opposed to 7 percent), while at the same time the percentage of jobs requiring no qualifications was decreasing.[41]

SENSE OF SOCIAL EXCLUSION

In terms of their experience, 89 percent of the respondents in the Cheshire Disability Review reported that there was discrimination and prejudice toward people with disabilities in the UK.[42] However, they felt steady improvement in physical accessibility to services such as shops, public transport or leisure facilities.

SOCIAL INCLUSION/EXCLUSION OF PEOPLE WITH DISABILITIES IN THE OECD

What is the status of social inclusion/social exclusion in the most developed countries? The expectation is that OECD countries will lean toward a high standard of social inclusion, at least with respect to income

---

[40] *Survey of English Housing*, Preliminary Report: 2007/08, CLG, 2009. Accessed 16 November 2011, http://www.communities.gov.uk/publications/corporate/statistics/sehpre limresults0708.

[41] Labour Force Survey: Employment status by occupation and sex, April–June 2007. Accessed 16 November 2011, http://www.ons.gov.uk/ons/search/index.html?pageSize= 50&newquery=Labour+Force+Survey+Employment+status+by+occupation+and+sex% 2C+April%E2%80%93June+2007.

[42] Leonard Cheshire Disability, *Disability poverty in the UK*, 46.

and employment indicators. An OECD report titled 'Transforming disability to ability: Policies to promote work and income security for disabled people'[43] provides an interesting picture of the status of people with disabilities in the most developed countries.

In terms of income, the publication demonstrates that OECD countries differ in income security. Income security in countries such as Austria, Denmark, Germany, the Netherlands, Sweden and Switzerland is reasonably high, as the household income for a family with a person with a disability almost matches the income of households without a person with a disability.[44] In the second category are countries such as Belgium, Canada, France, Italy, Norway and Canada where the relative income of households with a disabled person amounts to between 85 and 90 percent of households without a person with a disability. At the bottom are countries such as Portugal, Spain, the UK and the United States, where the income for households of a person with a disability is between 70 and 80 percent of the incomes of households without a person with a disability.[45] The cross-country benchmarks of income security are attributed to the different policies and disability benefit schemes in OECD countries or to the state of the economy in each country, including the rate of unemployment. Similar trends have been observed in personal income statistics.[46]

The report provides a fascinating insight into the importance of employment, as in most countries the earned income of working people with disabilities is only 5 to 15 percent lower than those without disabilities. Only in three countries – Sweden, the United States and Portugal – do people with disabilities earn 30-percent less income than people without disabilities. Cross-country absolute differences in employment rates of people with disabilities were larger than in relative terms. For example, in Norway and Switzerland, six out of ten working-age people with disabilities were employed, while the rate is two out of ten in countries such as Poland and Spain. Low employment rates can be related to high inactivity. The report reveals that the unemployment rate of people

[43] OECD, *Transforming disability into ability*.
[44] Ibid., pp. 28–32.
[45] Ibid., pp. 24–7.
[46] Ibid., pp. 26–7.

with disabilities in OECD countries is 80-percent higher than their coun-terparts (i.e., people without disabilities). Countries that have the highest gap (170 percent) are Austria, Germany and the Netherlands.[47]

The OECD findings highlight the importance of severity of disability. Overall, people with a severe disability have the highest rate of unem-ployment (180 percent) compared to people without a disability. A closer look at the findings shows that in Australia and Spain the differences in employment rates between people with severe and moderate disabilities were much smaller that on average, probably because of their slim chances of finding a job.

The analysis of these important indicators between OECD countries provides two important insights about income and employment of people with disabilities. The first is that indicators of social inclusion of people with disabilities, even in the most developed countries, are associated with particular economic realities and domestic social policies. Second, it is relatively difficult to provide an accurate picture of social inclusion of people with disabilities in these countries without paying attention to the severity of disability.

SOCIAL INCLUSION/EXCLUSION OF PEOPLE WITH DISABILITIES: THE NON-INDICATOR APPROACH

The earlier reports demonstrated that the common method of measuring social inclusion/social exclusion is to mix indicators taken from secondary data sources. However, social exclusion can be studied through the lens and experiences of people with disabilities.[48] A review of mental health studies reveals that people with psychiatric disabilities believed that their functioning was related to negative societal attitudes toward them, rather than to their own pathology.[49] Similarly, social inclusion is perceived as part of the recovery process. This section will provide a comprehensive review of research data that have explored the link between disability

---

[47] Ibid., pp. 23–56.
[48] Morgan et al., 'Social exclusion and mental health', 470–80.
[49] Liz Sayce, 'Stigma, discrimination and social exclusion: What's in a word?' *Journal of Mental Health* 7 (1998), 331–43.

and the labour market and two studies that will demonstrate the merit of the qualitative method to social exclusion of people with disabilities from Canada that has examined the experiences of people with disabilities in the workplace.[50] The second section is a national social participation study from Israel that examines the association between employment status and social participation of people with disabilities.[51]

IMPACT OF DISABILITY ON EMPLOYMENT AND DISABILITY BENEFITS: EVIDENCE FROM CORE RESEARCH STUDIES

There is growing empirical evidence that disability has a significant impact on the level of participation in the labour market and that there is prejudice toward those with severe psychiatric disabilities.[52] The focus has been on the discriminatory practices of employers that result in rejecting their employment.[53] The fact is that most of those with psychiatric disabilities are disproportionately poor, only a minority are in paid employment and many experience social isolation and limited leisure opportunities.

Other researchers are concerned about the effect of disability benefits on labour supply. Most of the studies consistently find a significant negative relationship between the two.[54] Specifically, the rise in disability claimants has been the result of a combination of a steady increase in disability benefits and the shortage of low-skilled and entry-level jobs. Unlike

---

[50] Rebecca Gewurtz and Bonnie Kirsh, 'Disruption, disbelief and resistance: A meta-synthesis of disability in the workplace', *Work: A Journal of Prevention, Assessment, and Rehabilitation* 34 (2009), 33–44.

[51] Arie Rimmerman and Tal Araten-Bergman, 'Employment and social participation among Israelis with disabilities', *Journal of Social Work Disability and Rehabilitation* 8 (2009), 132–45.

[52] Sayce, 'Stigma, discrimination and social exclusion', 331–4.

[53] Tania Burchardt, *Employment retention and the onset of sickness or disability: Evidence from the Labour Force Survey longitudinal datasets*, UK Department for Work and Pensions, In-house Report 109, 2003. Accessed 16 November 2011, http://www.start.co.il/search.aspx? q=Tania+Burchardt%2C+Employment+retention+and+the+onset+of+sickness+or+ disability%3A+Evidence+from+the+Labour+Force+Survey+longitudinal+datasets%2C+ UK+Department+for+Work+and+Pensions%2C+In-house+Report+109%2C+2003 .&cx=partner-pub-8811758745500993%3A1618419300&cof=FORID%3A11&ie=UTF-8&sa=%D7%97%D7%99%D7%A4%D7%95%D7%A9.

[54] See, for example, John Bound and Timothy Waidmann, 'Disability transfers, self-reported health and the labour attachment of older men: Evidence from the historical record', *The Quarterly Journal of Economics* 107 (1992), 1393–419.

the United States, the UK has not experienced falling real earnings at the lower end of the wage distribution and so benefit replacement rates have not been raised.

DISRUPTION, DISBELIEF AND RESISTANCE: A META-SYNTHESIS OF DISABILITY IN THE WORKPLACE[55]

Supporters of the social model of disability believe that disablement is grounded in the social environment and created through social interactions and interpretation. A similar perception applies to the workplace; that is, that integration in the workplace is determined by corporate culture and context. The meta-synthesis of seven qualitative studies presented below demonstrates how important organisational culture is in shaping the experiences of people with disabilities in the workplace. The seven qualitative studies used were carried out in the United States, Canada and the UK.[56] Three core findings were found that described the intersection

---

[55] Rebecca Gewurtz and Bonnie Kirsh, 'Disruption, disbelief and resistance: A meta-synthesis of disability in the workplace', *Work* 34 (2009), 33–44.

[56] Including the following studies: John Butterworth et al. in Massachusetts on eight adults with developmental disabilities who were working in a community-based job 'Workplace culture, social interactions, and supports for transition-age young adults', *Mental Retardation* 38 (2000), 342–353; Isabel Dyck and Lyn Jongbloed, 'Women with multiple sclerosis and employment issues: A focus on social and institutional environments', *Canadian Journal of Occupational Therapy* 67 (2000), 337–346 on thirty-one women with multiple sclerosis in British Columbia, Canada, working full- or part-time; Sharon L. Harlan and Pamela M. Robert, 'The social construction of disability in organizations: Why employers resist reasonable accommodation', *Work and Occupations* 25 (1998), 397–435 on fifty government employees with a broad range of physical and mental disabilities; Bonnie Kirsh, 'Work, workers, and workplaces: A qualitative analysis of narratives of mental health consumers', *Journal of Rehabilitation* 66 (2000), 24–30 on thirty-six consumers of mental health services in Ontario, Canada, who were either working six months in mainstream employment or had left their mainstream employment six months prior to recruitment; Ruth Pinder, 'Bringing back the body without blame?: The experience of ill and disabled people at work', *Sociology of Health & Illness* 17 (1995), 605–631 on two women with arthritis from London, UK; Louise Saint-Arnaud, Micheline Saint-Jean and Jean Damasse, 'Towards an enhanced understanding of factors involved in the return-to-work process of employees absent due to mental health problems', *Canadian Journal of Community Mental Health* 25 (2006), 303–315 on thirty-seven government employees from twelve departments of the Government of Quebec who had been absent from work due to their psychiatric disability; and finally, Muriel Westmorland et al., 'Perspectives on work (re)entry for persons with disabilities: Implications for clinicians', *Work* 18 (2002), 29–40 who carried out focus groups of eighty-six employees with disabilities, the majority of whom were from unionized environments. These studies provide unique

of the experience of disability and corporate culture: *disruption, disbelief* and *resistance.* Employers and supervisors viewed social accommodation as *disruptive* to the organisation, operation and structure of the workplace.

Disbelief reflects efforts to convince employers and other stockholders that people with disabilities are reliable and productive workers. Many workers with disabilities actively conceal their disability to protect their image of competency at work. On the other hand, in order to be eligible for accommodations and benefits, they have to disclose their disability. They are caught between their need for special accommodations and the fear that they will be labelled as troublemakers.

EMPLOYMENT AND SOCIAL PARTICIPATION AMONG ISRAELIS WITH DISABILITIES

Employment is a key facilitator of promoting social participation of people with disabilities.[57] Employment skills and career goals strengthen self-confidence, self-esteem and subsequently enhance community engagement and integration. In addition, they facilitate social interaction with co-workers and engagement in social activities outside the work place.

Two major competing theoretical frameworks explain the relationship between employment and community participation – time allocation and social capital. The theory of time allocation perceives the individual as both a producer and consumer of time (a restricted resource). In order to maintain well-being and an adequate quality of life, the individual has to maintain appropriate equilibrium between the production and consumption of time and other tangible resources. Hence, the more time one dedicates to work, the less time one spends on quality commodities such as social activities in the community. It appears that economically successful employees tend to spend a large portion of their time at work and frequently complain that they lack adequate time and resources to develop their own social and family life.

---

approaches to understanding barriers to social inclusion of people with disabilities in the workplace.

[57] This information is based on the author's recent research with Tal Araten-Bergman.

An alternative theoretical explanation for the relationship between community participation and employment is related to capital,[58] which indicates tangible resources that produce new goods or are used for profit. However, over the years, economic and social scholars have broadened the term to address a person's skills and social relationships. Social capital, defined mainly as social networking and the opportunity to build up personal and social potential, is fundamentally important for both employment and community participation. Interpersonal contacts are also important when seeking and retaining employment.

Research on the relationship between social capital and disability is scarce. The literature often describes people with disabilities as dependent solely on their own natural support systems of friends and family members. Furthermore, due to lack of social networks, they hardly report any social contacts with co-workers.

Rimmerman and Araten-Bergman[59] examined whether employment was positively correlated to social participation and wanted to identify the perceived barriers using a random national sample of 597 non-institutionalised, working-age Israelis with disabilities. The instrumentation used in the survey was the same as that employed by the National Organization on Disability (NOD) Harris Survey of Community Participation, with slight modifications to the language and context for use in Israel.

Core findings indicated that employed people with disabilities were significantly more integrated into social and civic activities than the unemployed. While most of the unemployed attributed their restricted patterns of participation to the lack of adequate financial resources, accessible transportation and encouragement from community organisations, the employed reported lack of time as their main barrier. The above findings suggest that employment and rich community participation patterns may reinforce each other and may serve as a useful vehicle for promoting social integration for people with disabilities in their communities.

---

[58] See opening section in this chapter on the interrelations between social inclusion/social exclusion and social capital.

[59] Rimmerman and Araten-Bergman, 'Employment and social participation among Israelis with disabilities', 132–6.

CONCLUSION

This chapter indicates that social inclusion and social exclusion have many faces. In Europe, social exclusion is generally viewed as disadvantageously related to poverty and certain norms of social, economic or political activity and applies to individuals, households, spatial areas or population groups. As such, it is measured by mixed relative indicators that demonstrate the gap between excluded subpopulations and the rest of society on a national basis. However, there is also a relative subjective interpretation of social exclusion through the experiences of deprivation of excluded subpopulations and groups. This approach is often associated with studies of stigma and non-indicative measures.

Research on social inclusion and social exclusion of people with disabilities is fairly new. Most of the new studies offer selective relative indicators to measure the gaps between people with and without disabilities domestically and internationally. The core indicators used in these studies are education, income, employment, and civic and social participation. They have shown that people with disabilities lag significantly behind with respect to these indicators. The non-indicators approach is less prevalent and used sporadically by social scientists and disability studies by academics as well as by specialists and advocates in mental health. These studies express the relative deprivation felt by people with disabilities in different communities.

4   MEDIA AND DISABILITY, DISABILITY CULTURE, AND DIGITAL DIVIDE

Chapter 2 provides a comprehensive historical overview on social exclusion of people with disabilities from ancient to modern times.[1] These individuals were portrayed as characters and bizarre objects of ridicule in societies that were fascinated by their abnormalities.[2] They were displayed at freak shows to amuse the public and were used to draw a clear line between people with disabilities and the public at large. Their negative images and stereotypes were transferred from distant history to the media of the twentieth century.

Culture and media culture are central dimensions of the construction of disability. Classical literature transmits negative interpretations and 'handicapism' of people with disabilities. However, the digital and printed media have the most important roles in influencing public opinion and attitudes in their portrayals of people with disabilities as deficient.[3]

IMAGES OF DISABILITY IN CLASSICAL LITERATURE

Books, especially classics, are powerful tools through which civilisations transform values and norms. They are often translated into numerous languages and become popular movies and TV programmes.

---

[1] Henri-Jacques Stiker, *A history of disability*. Translated by David T. Mitchell (Ann Arbor: University of Michigan Press, 1999), pp. 1–22.

[2] See David Gerber, 'Volition and valorization: The "careers" of people exhibited in freak shows'. In *Freakery: Cultural spectacles of the extraordinary body*. Edited by Rosemarie Garland Thomson (New York: New York University Press, 1996).

[3] See Gerard Goggin and Christopher Newell, *Digital disability: The social construction of disability in new media* (Oxford: Rowman and Littlefield, 2003).

Unfortunately, books that are classics use traditional images and roles of people with disabilities. Most of them provide negative images and present a range of distorted figures, such as the sinister hump of Richard III, the evil prosthesis of Captain Hook, the fear-inducing, thumping wooden leg of Captain Ahab and the pitiable crutch of Tiny Tim.[4] Another illustration of a powerful image of a person with intellectual disability is Lenny in John Steinbeck's *Of Mice and Men*, who is portrayed as a killer of living things, including a young woman, because he is not aware of his own strength.[5]

One of the most distorted stereotypes in the literature for conveying evil or disparagement is the 'twisted mind in the twisted body'. Authors of classical books often used the device of the 'deformed' outer body as a reflection of the distorted inner qualities of the characters of people with disabilities.[6] Shakespeare's literature demonstrates these stereotypes: Richard III is viewed as a sinister and evil person with a disability, who is guilty of ruthless murder – even of children – to achieve his ends. Charles Dickens portrayed Quilp in *The Old Curiosity Shop* as an evil, lame dwarf, and, similarly, Victor Hugo described Quasimodo in *The Hunchback of Notre-Dame* as the 'twisted mind in the twisted body'.

However, the image of disability in the classical literature can be presented as pitiful and not necessarily as evil. These images are associated with Christian and Old Testament beliefs that disabled people are helpless and may be cured by the able-bodied. Good illustrations of this are crippled Tiny Tim in *A Christmas Carol*, who represents a symbol of innocence and hope and who finally makes Scrooge mend his ways, and Clara, a wealthy crippled girl who is cured by the heroine in Johanna Spyri's *Heidi*.[7]

IMAGES OF DISABILITY IN THE MEDIA

Historically, media portrayals of people with disabilities have clustered around two visible stereotypes: (1) evil and mentally ill villains or

---

[4] Howard Margolis and Arthur Shapiro, 'Countering negative images of disability in classical literature', *English Journal* 75 (1987), 18–22.
[5] Ibid.
[6] Ibid.
[7] Ibid.

(2) superheroes who can beat any obstacle.[8] These depicted stereotypes are paternalistic as they distort and provide unrealistic and recurring figures. The most comprehensive study on disabling imagery in the media was carried out in the UK by Colin Barnes, who identified several stereotypes that were common in the British media.[9]

The *pitiable* and *pathetic* are often portrayed in TV charity shows and telethons. They try to raise money for a specific disability or incurable illness by building heartbreaking stories or scenes of dependent and helpless figures with disabilities in need of help. A good example is the controversy about Jerry Lewis's Muscular Dystrophy Association (MDA) Telethon.[10] Many disability rights activists have organised actions against the Jerry Lewis MDA Labor Day Telethon because they felt that the annual telethon relied on 'the pity approach' to raise money for the Muscular Dystrophy Association and undermined the message of the disability civil rights movement for millions of viewers each year.

The disabled person as an *object of violence* is rooted in historical images taken from the Ancient Greeks (infanticide), medieval Europe (witchcraft) and the nineteenth and early-twentieth centuries (eugenics). Barnes demonstrated that the characters of people with disabilities were three times more likely to die by the end of TV shows than non-disabled characters.[11] Another illustration portraying a blind woman as a victim appeared in the classical thriller *Wait until Dark*,[12] in which Audrey Hepburn played a young blind woman whose husband unknowingly brought home a little doll full of cocaine. Very soon three criminals, one of them a dangerous psychopath, invade her house to retrieve the doll and she has to fight for her life. The film used her blindness to build tension in the movie and make her helplessness and panic more believable. Alternatively, she must be experienced enough to fight against the attackers and be competent and relaxed around her home so that her blindness would not steal attention from the plot.[13]

[8] Susan S. Eberly, 'Fairies and folklore of disability: Changelings, hybrids and the solitary fairy', *Folklore* 99 (1988), 58–75.

[9] Colin Barnes, *Disabling imagery and the media: An exploration of the principles for media representations of disabled people* (Halifax: BCODP/Ryburn Publishing, 1992).

[10] *The Kids Are All Right*: documentary Web site about a former Jerry's Kid named Mike Ervin. Accessed 22 November 2011 at http://www.thekidsareallright.org/.

[11] Barnes, *Disabling imagery and the media*.

[12] Ibid.

[13] Ibid.

The image of a *sinister* and *evil* presence is the most persistent stereo-type and is associated with historical portrayals. People with disabilities are considered as operating outside the normative rules of society and there-fore must be controlled or destroyed. *Moby Dick* is a classical example: Captain Ahab becomes so obsessed by the white whale's destruction of one of his legs that he sacrifices himself and most of his crew in pursuit of revenge.[14] Herman Melville uses the physical impairment to heighten the sinister atmosphere of the book.

The use of a person with a disability in creating *atmosphere* or *curio* is quite common in the media. A typical illustration is the animated feature *The Hunchback of Notre Dame* from Walt Disney. The story is adapted from the 1831 classic French novel by Victor Hugo in which the main character and hero of the tale is Quasimodo (a derogatory name mean-ing 'half-formed', given to him by his evil adoptive father Judge Claude Follo), a man with physical deformities who is imprisoned in the bell tower of the Notre Dame Cathedral in Paris. The story traces his early, troubled beginnings following the murder of his gypsy parents and his later departure from his oppressive living conditions to become integrated into everyday society. There is no doubt that by portraying Quasimodo as a 'freak' or monster, the film sends a clear message that people with disabilities are marginal in society.

Another use of this stereotype as curio is evident in 'freak shows', which were very popular during the rise of the eugenics movement in the United States. They exhibited freaks of nature, unusually deformed men and women who performed in a bizarre way that was shocking to the audience. There is no doubt that the shows provided the audience with disability voyeurism and a sense that these peculiar and exotic people were immoral and different from the rest of us.

The *super cripple* image is known in the popular literature as the 'super-crip' stereotype, a term used by people studying disabled narratives to describe courageous people with disabilities coping successfully with their disabilities against the odds. The basic assumption is that someone with a serious disability is doomed to be incapable of doing much.[15] This

---

[14] Howard Margolis and Arthur Shapiro, 'Countering negative images of disability in classical literature', *English Journal* 75 (1987), 18–22.

[15] Douglas Biklen, 'The culture of policy: Disability images and their analogues in public policy', *Social Problems* 15 (1987), 515–35.

perception is based on the common belief that people with disabilities fail to cope with their hardship unless they overcome it.[16] Those who overcome their destiny are perceived as heroes, sending a clear message to most of the people with disabilities that they are losers or have not tried hard enough. Perhaps the most famous symbol of such a hero is U.S. President Franklin Delano Roosevelt, who perceived himself as 'cured cripple' even though he could not walk at all.[17]

Another famous person who was portrayed as a supercrip was the actor Christopher Reeve, whose most famous movie role was that of Superman. Following a horseback-riding accident in 1995 that left him a quadriplegic until his death in 2004, he remained absolutely committed to regaining his ability to walk. Reeve even allowed himself to be digitally remastered to seemingly 'walk' in a 2000 Super Bowl commercial aimed at getting people to donate money to spinal cord research. In his words, 'We were not meant to be living in wheelchairs. We were meant to be walking upright with all our body systems fully functional, and I'd like to have that back . . . I'm not that interested in lower sidewalks', he told a reporter. It was nice to have access, he said, but people with disabilities should regard those disabilities 'as a temporary setback rather than a way of life'.[18] Reeve was perceived as controversial in the disability community as some believed he highlighted their inferior status as second-class citizens.[19]

The stereotype of an *object of ridicule* or *fool* is rooted in Ancient Greek and Roman history. Historically, people with disabilities were a source of amusement for non-disabled people. People with disabilities were and still are used in 'freak shows' or as cartoon characters with comical speech and sight problems. Modern examples are the ridiculed Porky Pig who stutters and is portrayed as cognitively challenged and mentally unhealthy, and Mr. Magoo, an elderly cartoon character with a visual impairment that walks into walls. The two characters amuse children and audiences at the expense of people with disabilities.

However, the mockery of people with disabilities is still being presented in movies such as *Tropic Thunder*, a fairly recent big-budget comedy

---

[16] Mary Johnson, 'The media ignores people with disabilities', *Utne Reader* 56 (1993), 106.
[17] Ibid., 117.
[18] Ibid., 128–9.
[19] Ibid.

made by DreamWorks/Paramount and directed and co-written by Ben Stiller, who also takes the leading role. The movie plot centres on a group of pampered actors who are lost in the jungle while making a war movie. Stiller's character, Tugg Speedman, is presented as a fading action hero who earlier failed in his bid for Oscar glory for his portrayal of Simple Jack, a character with an intellectual disability. Speedman as Simple Jack is featured as a movie within the movie. The plot involving Simple Jack and Stiller's portrayal of the character occupy close to thirty minutes of screen time. In character, Stiller speaks in a stilted, stuttering, adenoidal fashion and wears overalls, bad false teeth and a classic, institutional bowl haircut. There are many instances of the use of the word 'retard' and its variations; there are least sixteen instances in the 'full retard' scene, not counting the uses of words such as 'idiot', 'moron', 'moronical', 'imbecile', 'stupid' and 'dumb', all of which are used to describe the character of Simple Jack, who is described in an introductory segment as a 'mentally impaired farm hand who can talk to animals'.[20]

Portraying a person with disability as his or her *own worst enemy* is another stereotype that is associated with the traditional medical model. The latter portrays people with disabilities as responsible for their lives. If they follow a professional's prescription and demonstrate independence and compliance, they may succeed. There are two well-known films that represent this image: *Coming Home* and *Born on the Fourth of July*. The heroes of both films are veterans coping with disabilities caused by war.

The common metaphor of disability presented in these movies is of dependency and vulnerability. *Coming Home* features the story of a woman (Jane Fonda) whose husband is fighting in Vietnam. She falls in love with a disabled veteran suffering paralysis and loss of masculinity. The ex-husband, who suffered from mental illness as a result of the war, commits suicide. *Born on the Fourth of July* is the biography of Ron Kovic, who was paralysed in the Vietnam War and became an antiwar

---

[20] *Tropic Thunder* was criticised by the disability advocacy community. Timothy Shriver, the chairman of the Special Olympics, stated, 'This population struggles too much with the basics to have to struggle against Hollywood. We're sending a message that this hate speech is no longer acceptable'. See Lang Derrick, 'Mental disability groups protest "Tropic Thunder"' *USA Today*, 12 August 2008. Accessed at http://www.webcitation.org/5u540ERuV.

and pro-human rights political activist after successful sexual encounters with Mexican prostitutes.

The *person with disability as a burden* is probably the most obvious stereotype, and it portrays people with disabilities as helpless, dependent and in need of ongoing care by people without disabilities. This image has its roots in the history of people with disabilities. The Greeks and the Romans differentiated between productive and unproductive people with disabilities, justifying the neglect and even the extermination of those who are a burden on society.[21] Similarly, the eugenics movement and the Nazis practised euthanasia on people with disabilities, justifying the need to get rid of those who could not fit in and might be a burden on society.[22]

Images of people with disabilities as a burden on society and dependent on ongoing care often appear in advertising campaigns to attract public support and donations. In his book *No Pity: People with Disabilities Forging a New Civil Rights Movement*, Joseph P. Shapiro argues that 'The poster child is a sure-fire tug at our hearts. The children picked to represent charity fund-raising drives are brave, determined and inspirational, the most innocent victims of the cruellest whims of life and health. Yet they smile through their "unlucky" fates – a condition that weakens muscles or cuts life expectancy to a brutish handful of years, a birth "defect" or childhood trauma. No other symbol of disability is more beloved by Americans than the cute and courageous poster child – or more loathed by people with disabilities themselves'.[23]

A close look at the Easter Seals poster stamps from 1934 to 1944 demonstrates the images of innocence, dependency and neediness. The posters sent a clear message that society could cure children if donations were available. Very little changed between 1945 and 1952; the image of helpless 'crippled' children is evident on the stamps. There is an expectation that public support will reduce, to some extent, their dependency. Only the mid-1950s (1953–1957) mark a change in the image of 'crippled' children. The traditional stereotypes are replaced by symbols of hope.

---

[21] Stiker, *A history of disability*, pp. 24–130.

[22] See Udo Benzenhöfer, *Euthanasia in Germany before and during the Third Reich* (Münster: Klemm & Oelschläger, 2010).

[23] Joseph P. Shapiro, *No pity: People with disabilities forging a new civil rights movement* (New York: Three Rivers Press, 1994), p. 12.

Easter Seals Poster Stamps 1934–1944

Easter Seals Poster Stamps 1945–1952

Easter Seals Poster Stamps 1953–1957

The *asexual* or *sexually abnormal image* is a stereotype that exists in old and new media. The traditional message is that people with disabilities are asexual and therefore their lives are worthless.[24] An early movie, *The*

24 Kim Eunjung, 'Asexuality in disability narratives', *Sexualities* 14 (2011), 479–93.

Men, tells the story of Ken Wilocek, a soldier whose spine was shattered at the end of the war by a German sniper. Paralysed from the waist down, he had to struggle to be a man despite his handicap. The film portrays the belief that people with disabilities are asexual and have to cope with their destiny.[25] A similar stereotype of a person with a disability coping with his masculinity appears in a newer film, *The Waterdance*.[26] Eric Stoltz stars as a young writer left incapacitated by a hiking accident. He is placed in a paraplegic ward occupied by patients of all races and emotional conditions. Together with his newfound friends, Stoltz rebels against the hospital system and his own debilitation.

Another angle of the theme of asexuality in Hollywood movies is of parents denying the sexuality of their children with disabilities. In the film *The Other Sister*, Carla, a teenager with an intellectual disability, has just returned home after several years in an institution. Her ambition is to train as a veterinarian's assistant. Her overprotective mother denies her daughter's desire to be independent, to date and to have sex.[27] In *The Idiots*, Stoffer, a spoilt brat living gratis in his uncle's house under the pretext of preparing it for sale, invites a bunch of friends over to stay. Without any money to get by, Stoffer comes upon the idea of 'spazzing', that is, the group pretends to be intellectually disabled in order to avail themselves of society's generosity. What starts out as a joke quickly becomes a way of life for him and his commune as they try to 'get in touch with their inner idiot' by constantly 'spazzing'.[28] The film portrays the image of people with intellectual disabilities as sexually abnormal by showing them involved in an outrageous, hardcore orgy.

The *person with disability as lacking social participation* is a common stereotype in Western media. The rare visibility of characters with disabilities in the media gives the impression that people with disabilities have difficulty participating in society or that their appearance has to be avoided in order to protect them. Both interpretations mean denial of their recognition in popular culture. Morris explains that disability in the media has become 'a metaphor . . . for the message that the non-disabled

---

[25] *The Men* is a 1950s film directed by Fred Zinnemann.
[26] *The Waterdance* is a 1992 film directed by Eric Stoltz.
[27] *The Other Sister* is a 1999 film directed by Garry Marshall.
[28] *The Idiots* is a 1998 Danish film directed by Lars von Trier.

writer wishes to get across, in the same way that "beauty" is used. In doing this, the writer draws on the prejudice, ignorance and fear that generally exist toward disabled people, knowing that to portray a character with a humped back, with a missing leg, with facial scars, will evoke certain feelings in the reader or audience. The more disability is used as a metaphor for evil, or just to induce a sense of unease, the more the cultural stereotype is confirmed'.[29]

An interesting perspective on the media was offered in a recent book *The Problem Body: Projecting Disability on Film*, edited by Sally Chivers and Nicole Markotić.[30] Based on the work of eleven leading disability scholars from the United States, the UK, Canada and South Korea on 'the problem body' in films, the authors concluded that disability exists in movies in many ways but is hardly recognised socially or culturally.

This interpretation is confirmed in a fairly new report on minority representation on broadcast television.[31] According to the report, scripted characters with disabilities represented only 1 percent of all scripted series regular characters – 6 characters out of 587 – on the 5 broadcast networks: ABC, CBS, The CW, FOX and NBC. Although people with disabilities are largely absent from the television scene, they are very present in the American scene. The U.S. Census Bureau found in their 2008 survey that slightly more than 12 percent of U.S. citizens reported an apparent disability.[32]

Portraying *Persons with Disabilities as Normal* is a fairly recent image and consonant with a human rights perspective. This change was seen on TV in *Life Goes On*, one of the many successful shows to have received public acceptance, in which Christopher Burke featured an actor with Down syndrome.[33] In the 1990s, television commercials often showed someone in a wheelchair or with a physical disability carrying on a happy life and socially involved. However, these images were the exception, as

---

[29] Jenny Morris, *Pride against prejudice* (London: Women's Press, 1991), p. 93.

[30] Sally Chivers and Nicole Markotić, *The problem body: Projecting disability on film* (Columbus: Ohio State University Press, 2010).

[31] Gay & Lesbian Alliance Against Defamation (GLAAD), *Where we are on TV report: 2010–2011*. Accessed 11 November 2011 at www.glaad.org.

[32] U.S. Census Bureau: 2008 American Community Survey. Accessed at http://www.census .gov/acs/www/.

[33] *Life Goes On* was a television series that aired on ABC network from 12 September 1989 to 23 May 1993.

most of the images portrayed were biased. Probably the most progressive image of disability was presented in *Sesame Street*, an educational TV programme that received numerous international awards.[34] A few episodes that portrayed disability as normal appeared in the 1980s and 1990s. Among the most remarkable episodes is *The Clapping Song*, in which Gordon, one of the regular cast members on *Sesame Street*, sings a song about clapping with Big Bird and a group of children, one of whom is using a wheelchair – no big deal or mention about disability; it is not a particularly dynamic segment, perhaps because Gordon does not seem to 'engage' the children in any special way.[35]

In *Sesame Street*'s *My Dad Racing in His Wheelchair*, a young girl introduces her dad who is a racer and uses a wheelchair. He calls her his coach, and she helps and encourages him in training and cheers him on in the real race. After the race, she hops on his chair for a ride and he thanks his 'coach'.[36] And, finally, consider Dee Schur's *From Your Head* song with Elmo, one of the Muppets. Elmo asks Dee Schur what she is doing and she explains that she is reading Braille because she is blind. He asks her how she learns about things and she simply explains that in addition to Braille, she hears, feels and smells (and that she likes the monster way Elmo smells). Then she sings a song about one of the most important ways one knows about things: through the *ideas that come from your head*. Elmo and Dee have a nice rapport and the song is simple and clear.[37]

IMAGES OF DISABILITY IN THE PRINTED MEDIA

There is no doubt that the coverage of disability in the printed media is stereotypical, paternalistic and inaccurate.[38] In the printed media, there

---

[34] Shalom M. Fisch, Rosemarie T. Truglio and Charlotte F. Cole, 'The impact of Sesame Street on preschool children: A review and synthesis of 30 years' research', *Media Psychology* 1 (2009), 165–90.

[35] Barbara Kolucki, 'Sesame Street Continues to be a Winner', *Disability World* 9 (2001). Accessed 1 November 2011 at http://www.disabilityworld.org/11–12_02/arts/sesamestreet.shtml.

[36] Ibid.

[37] Ibid.

[38] See, for example, early work by Douglas Biklen, 'Framed: Print journalism's treatment of disability issues', in Allen Gartner and Tom Joe, *Images of the disabled: Disabling images* (New

are traditional issues covered by newspapers such as budget expenditures, housing and institutional care that are considered to be more influential than hard news.[39] Leading newspapers such as *The New York Times* and the *Washington Post* were found to be progressive with respect to the political, cultural and civic rights of deaf people.

However, when covering general news, the newspapers used traditional stereotypes. One of the interesting studies on newspapers that examined the sixteen most prestigious and highly circulated daily newspapers in the United States over a period of three months found that the traditional perspective was prevalent, but it was not associated with a negative portrayal of disability.[40] A fairly recent study conducted in Australia showed that people with disabilities tend to receive little coverage in the Australian media. Coverage, when it does occur, is often misguided and helps to perpetuate negative stereotypes. The pilot study on the coverage of disability in the *Adelaide Advertiser*, a large daily newspaper, found that fewer than 20 percent of the articles that appeared in the newspaper conveyed people with disabilities in a positive way. The most problematic finding was that all opinion articles were identified as negative.[41]

In order to provide an in-depth international perspective on the role of the printed media in portraying progressive images of people with disabilities, I introduce here three of my recent studies – two from Israel and one from the United States. The first is 'The power of the powerless: A study of the Israeli disability strike of 1999';[42] the second is a recent study called 'Media and the Israeli disability rights legislation: Progress or mixed and contradictory images?';[43] and the third is current research

York: Praeger, 1987), pp. 36–47; and Anne M. Cooke and Neil H. Reisner, 'The last minority American', *Journalism Review* (1991).

[39] Ronald K. Yoshida, Lynn Wasilewski and Douglas L. Friedman, 'Recent newspaper coverage about persons with disabilities', *Exceptional Children* 56 (1990), 418–23.

[40] John. S. Clogston, 'Reporters' attitudes toward and newspaper coverage of persons with disabilities', unpublished Ph.D. thesis, Michigan State University (1991).

[41] Kerry Green and Stephan Tanner, 'Reporting disability', *Asia Pacific Media Educator* 19 (2009), 43–54.

[42] Arie Rimmerman and Stanley S. Herr, 'The power of the powerless', 12–18.

[43] Michal Soffer, Arie Rimmerman, Peter Blanck and Eve Hill, 'Media and the Israeli disability rights legislation: Progress or mixed and contradictory images?' *Disability & Society* 25 (2010), 687–99.

on 'Representations of ADA employment-related issues in *The Wall Street Journal* (1990–2008)'.[44]

The first study examined Israeli press coverage of the disability rights movement in terms of participants, demands and political response. The secondary purpose of this research was to examine whether the coverage reflected progressive or traditional perspectives. The researchers analysed fifty reports and articles published in the three leading daily newspapers (*Yedioth Ahronoth*, *Maariv* and *Haaretz*) between 18 October 1999 and 8 February 2000. The findings revealed that although the press perceived the strike as a general one, it mainly cited people with mobility disabilities, minimising the presence of other disability groups. This mixed message was also evident in reflecting the demands of the demonstrators: While the headlines overtly reflected disability rights, the texts emphasised demands for benefits. This was observed also in the government's response in that it negotiated with the protesters regarding benefits rather than civil rights issues. In terms of the secondary purpose of the study, it is clear that the press reflected a traditional perspective of the protesters. Their dominant image was of a weak and painful group of sufferers rather than activists.[45]

The second study[46] examined the following questions: Do the Israeli printed media express the nature and spirit of the 'Equal Rights for Persons with Disabilities Law' legislation? What are the portrayals and metaphors of people with disabilities in the Israeli printed media and do they reflect the expected changes and realities in terms of civic participation and inclusion in society?

Findings have shown a clear discrepancy between new disability terminology and conceptualisation as they appear in the Israeli Equal Rights for Persons with Disabilities Law of 1998 and the media's representation of disability. Unfortunately, the printed media reflect mixed and contradictory images of conceptualisations, a tangle of biomedical and welfare regulations dictating treatment and rehabilitation regimes, alongside other legislation and practices that emphasise rights and equality. In terms of

---

[44] Michal Soffer and Arie Rimmerman, 'Representations of ADA employment-related issues in *The Wall Street Journal* (1990–2008)', *International Journal of Rehabilitation Research* 35 (2012), 184–186.

[45] Rimmerman and Herr, 'The power of the powerless', 14–17.

[46] Soffer et al., 'Media and the Israeli disability rights legislation', 687–99.

portrayals and metaphors of people with disabilities, this study examined and validated similar research on media representations of illness and disability that were conducted in other Western countries. For example, contemporary research shows usage of military metaphors to describe severe diseases (such as cancer) in various media. In addition, findings indicated that persons with disabilities are portrayed as victims or pitiful, dangerous 'others' and/or supercrips.

The two Israeli studies demonstrated that the printed media view people with disabilities in a paradoxical way. On the one hand, there is recognition of the rights of people with disabilities and awareness of progressive legislation. On the other hand, in terms of description of events or reporting, there are traces of the traditional images and metaphors.

The third study[47] provides an opportunity to examine the situation in the United States. The explorative research looked at how *The Wall Street Journal*, one of the leading economic newspapers in the United States, covers employment-related issues that derive from the ADA of 1990. The researchers carried out quantitative and qualitative content analysis of thirty-nine newspaper articles that were published in *The Wall Street Journal* in 1990, 2000 and 2008. The findings suggest mixed messages: Although some negative representations of disability seem to have declined throughout the years, others, no less problematic, have surfaced. A central finding concerns the emergence of a legal-administrative discourse of disability whereby disability, which was once seen simply as a social burden, is currently seen as a fiscal burden on employers that is mandated by the state. This image stands in contrast to the spirit of the ADA and to the perception of disability as a civil rights matter.

HOLLYWOOD FILM'S ROLES IN PORTRAYING PEOPLE WITH DISABILITIES

Oscar critic Emanuel Levy thinks that Hollywood is an image-making machine and a dictionary of diseases, both physical and mental. He lists popular movies: *As Good as It Gets, Avatar, A Beautiful Mind, Forrest Gump, My Left Foot, Rain Man* and *Scent of a Woman*. He believes that

---

[47] Soffer and Rimmerman, 'Representations of ADA employment-related issues'.

these worthy movies about addiction, alcoholism, amnesia, autism, blindness, disfigurement and paraplegia are sacrificial offerings to the movie muse, so that the studios can continue to make frivolous films that celebrate youth, speed and beauty.[48] Similarly, film professor Martin F. Norden surveyed the portrayal of physically disabled characters in mainstream American cinema over the last hundred years. He sees cinema images of disability as reflecting society's view of disabled people and believes all disabled characters are shaped by the isolation of disabled people as a group in society. This is apparent not only in the storylines of the films, but also in the framing, editing and sounding. These films then make their own contribution to perpetuating and reinforcing that isolation.[49]

However, the number of Academy Award–winning films portraying individuals with disabilities has dramatically increased since the Academy Awards were first handed out in 1929. These movies reflect the trend that people with disabilities are becoming more visible members in Western society, which is particularly evident in the high frequency of portrayals of those with psychiatric disabilities.[50] The results demonstrated that from 1928 to 1937 only one award depicted a person with a disability in a major role compared to nine films from 1990 to 1996. Fifty-four percent of the films portrayed psychiatric disturbances, by far the most common type of disability depicted in the films, followed by physical disabilities, sensory disabilities, mental retardation and autism.[51]

Stereotypes of people with psychiatric disabilities reflect the 'imagery of madness', violence, suspense and drama. For example, the film *The Silence of the Lambs* won Best Picture, Best Actor and Best Actress in 1991 for its depiction of serial killers. It is hardly a rendition of reality, as statistics indicate there are only about four to five instances of serial killers in the United States per year. Similarly, Dustin Hoffman's portrayal in *Rain Man* (1988) of Raymond, an incredible autistic idiot savant capable of completing acts of genius such as astonishing memorisation and solving

[48] Emanuel Levy, *All about Oscar: The history and politics of the Academy Award* (New York: Continuum, 2003).

[49] Martin F. Norden, *The cinema of isolation: A history of physical disability in the movies* (New Brunswick: Rutgers University Press, 1994).

[50] Steve P. Sofran, 'Disability portrayal in film: Reflecting the past, directing the future', *Teaching Exceptional Children* 64 (1998), 227–38.

[51] Ibid., 231–3.

complicated mathematical problems quickly. The image is a distortion of reality because very few autistic people are savants.

Lisa Lopez Levers provides a qualitative study[52] of the treatment of mental illness in twenty-one selected Hollywood films involving scenes of psychiatric hospitalisation and spanning the half-century from the 1940s through the 1980s. Basing her qualitative analysis on Gilman's work, Levers found that persons with a psychiatric disability were largely depicted as dangerous on the one hand and as passive objects of violence on the other, as medically pathological and as pathetic or comical figures, whose stereotypical representations in most films create a pathological or deviant atmosphere.[53] Most of the frequently appearing icons illustrated either the dangerous stereotype (staff/club, restrained, held/guided by warders, body invasive technique and cage) or the object of violence/passive stereotype (eyes cast down, hiding hands, seated, restrained, scampering fools, held/guided by warders, body invasive technique and cage).

Portrayals of 'madness' are far from reflecting the reality of a psychiatric impairment. The concern is that this powerful visual representation shapes and reshapes the perceptions of the public. There is a need therefore to facilitate a better understanding of the deep structure of the stereotype of madness, a structure rooted in centuries of mistreatment.

DISABILITY CULTURE

Irving Zola, a leading scholar in the sociology of disability, thought that people with disabilities were different from other minority groups with respect to their social recognition and culture.[54] Although most members of minority groups grow up in a recognised subculture and share common norms and identities, people with disabilities are born or acquire disability or illness without being aware of their special conditions. They often experience societal denial of disability and have to experience prejudice and social exclusion. Therefore, their struggle to form

---

[52] Lisa Lopez Levers, 'Representations of psychiatric disability in fifty years of Hollywood film: An ethnographic analysis', *Theory and Science* (2001). Accessed 12 September 2011 at http://theoryandscience.icaap.org/content/vol002.002/lopezlevers.html.

[53] See Sander L. Gilman, *Seeing the insane* (New York: Wiley, 1982).

[54] Irving K. Zola, 'Self, identity and the naming question: Reflections on the language of disability', *Social Science & Medicine* 36 (1993), 167–73.

identity and language has been belated, as disability culture is a fairly new conceptualisation.

Disability culture can be interpreted as a sense of common identity and common interests that position people with disabilities as separate from others. Consequently, this culture reflects a shared sense of exclusion, with different group expressions of social and political consciousness.[55] Does disability culture express solidarity of all people with impairments? The case of deaf culture, which is presented in the next section, is a clear example of a differentiation of disability groups. Furthermore, historically, most of the disability communities in the Western world have emerged from segregated medicalised groups.

The discussion about the existence of disability culture is fascinating. Susan Peters, who raised the question of whether there is a disability culture, suggested three options for establishing cultural identity: (1) refigure the difference inherent in the other (by stepping outside); (2) focus on the other to create oppositional identity and (3) produce cultural meaning and subjectivity of your own image.[56] She goes on to outline the 'many cultures of disability' that exist as a function of different worldviews and argues that a synchronisation of these perspectives can provide an understanding of disability culture as 'a thriving cross-cultural phenomenon which knows no national boundaries' that 'allows for an individual hybrid consciousness which maintains tactical solidarity while not being swallowed up by universal cultural patterns and norms'.[57]

THE CASE OF DEAF CULTURE

Is deafness considered a disability or a culture? Over the past few decades, self-advocates and leading professionals have argued that deafness is not pathological and therefore does not need to be 'fixed'.[58] Proponents of deafness as a culture distinguish deaf culture by using the capital

---

[55] Colin Barnes and Geoff Mercer, 'Disability culture: Assimilation or inclusion?' In *Handbook of disability studies*. Edited by Gary L. Albrecht, Katherine D. Seelman and Michael Bury (Thousand Oaks: Sage, 2003), pp. 515–34.

[56] Susan Peters, 'Is there a disability culture? A syncretization of three possible world views', *Disability and Society* 15 (1980), 583–601.

[57] Ibid., 597, 583, 585.

[58] See for example, Ruth Butler, Tracy Skelton and Gill Valentine, 'Language barriers: Exploring the world of the deaf', *Disability Studies Quarterly* 21 (2001), 42–52; or Carol Padden and

'D' whereas the lower case 'd' signifies deafness as a pathology.[59] The rationale is that an individual who cannot hear is potentially a member of a rich cultural heritage that separates the individual from non-Deaf members in their families or communities. Edward Dolnick's article, 'Deafness as Culture', presents an excellent summary of the deaf culture debate. 'Parent and child belong to different cultures, as they would in an adoption along racial lines', says Dolnick, 'And deaf children acquire a sense of cultural identity from their peers rather than their parents'.[60]

Other scholars defined culture as 'a set of learned behaviours of a group of people who have their own language, values, rules for behaviours and traditions'.[61] Deaf people behave similarly, use the same language and share the same beliefs. The view of deafness as culture holds that children and adults who cannot hear are isolated from the mainstream because communication with hearing individuals will always be laborious.

It is clear that those who use sign language as a first language constitute a linguistic minority. Sign language is seen as an expression of values that are carried across generations. Hence, sign language represents a cultural identity: 'many deaf people now proclaim they are a subculture like any other . . . a linguistic minority (speaking American Sign Language) . . . no more in a need of a cure for their condition than are Haitians or Hispanics'.[62] The use of sign language is the ticket to 'Deaf culture'; therefore, those who are not 'pure' signers are viewed as outsiders or members of the 'hearing world'. The basic belief is that only those who have acquired the use of sign language early in life and who use sign as their first language have an understanding of Deaf cultural norms. This perception can limit access to the culture by persons who desire to enter after childhood – for example, people who lose their hearing in adolescence or adulthood, or those who were raised with English as their first language but wish to learn sign language later in life.

The cochlear implants controversy originated in the early 1980s.[63] The dispute was between hearing and non-hearing parents of deaf

---

Tom Humphries, *Deaf in America: Voices from a culture* (Cambridge, MA: Harvard University Press, 1988).

[59] See Edward Dolnick, 'Deafness as culture', *The Atlantic Monthly* (Sept. 1993), 37–53.

[60] Ibid., 38.

[61] Padden and Humphries, *Deaf in America*, p. 4.

[62] Dolnick, 'Deafness as culture', 37.

[63] Shelli Delost and Sarah Lashley, 'The cochlear implant controversy'. Accessed 1 November 2010 at http://www.drury.edu/multinl/story.cfm?ID=2442&NLID=166.

children. Proponents of the cochlear implant supported the use of this technology, which can medically repair deafness in children with prelingual sensorineural hearing loss. Parents who decided to use this technology with their children have received massive support from the medical community and professional audiologist associations. The technology enables hearing parents to communicate with their children. Most of these parents reject the claims that they are motivated by a selfish desire to 'normalise' their children. However, many in the Deaf community argue that these children are caught between two worlds and will be further disadvantaged and marginalised in society. They view the cochlear implant as a threat to Deaf culture and an effort to rob this socio-cultural minority that is different but not deficient.

This culture clash is an interesting example of a population that chooses to segregate itself from the mainstream in order to preserve its culture. The Deaf community views cochlear implants as a threat to a child's self-esteem: A child who has received an implant is still labelled as disabled. The Deaf community believes that inclusion as a deaf person fosters pride.

DIGITAL DIVIDE AS A MAJOR BARRIER TO SOCIAL INCLUSION

Digital divide refers to the gap between those who can effectively use new information and communication technology (ICT) and those who cannot due to the lack of access and/or necessary skills.[64,65] While those 'information-haves' use technology to gain better education and jobs and to be more involved in the community, 'information have-nots' fall behind and in fact miss opportunities in an emerging information-based society.

---

[64] See for example, Neil Selwyn, 'Reconsidering political and popular understandings of the digital divide', *New Media & Society* 6 (2004), 341–62; Lisa J. Servon, *Bridging the digital divide: Technology, community and public policy* (Malden, MA: Blackwell, 2002); and U.S. Department of Commerce, *Falling through the net: Toward digital inclusion* (Washington, D.C.: National Telecommunications and Information Administration, 2000). Accessed at http://www.ntia.doc.gov/ntiahome/fttn00/contents00.html.

[65] Benjamin M. Compaine is senior research affiliate at the Internet and Telecoms Convergence Consortium at the Massachusetts Institute of Technology. He is the editor of *The digital divide: Facing a crisis or creating a myth?* (Cambridge, MA: The MIT Press, 2001).

From the political point of view, digital divide is interpreted as global divide, social divide and democratic divide.[66] The definition covers gaps of Internet access, which affect individual engagement, mobilisation and participation. The divide is interpreted by policy makers as a social problem derived from the intersection between social systems and communication technologies. In this sense, digital divide ceased being a matter of physical access to computers and connectivity and became a challenge in terms of content, language, education, literacy, or community and social resources.

Therefore, digital divide implies a chain of causality just as the lack of access to computers and the Internet is associated with fewer chances to succeed and prosper. While this point is undoubtedly true, the reverse is equally true: Those who are already marginalised will have fewer opportunities to access and use computers and the Internet. In fact, technology and society are intertwined and co-constitutive, and this complex interrelationship makes any assumption of causality problematic. As a result, any strategy or policy to bridge the digital divide has to be comprehensive and beyond physical access.

In one of the most comprehensive reports on digital divide, Teresa Peters and her staff argued that real disparities exist in access to and use of ICT between countries (the 'international digital divide') and between groups within countries (the 'domestic digital divide').[67] In fact, they predict that the digital gap will be wider in the future because privileged groups acquire and use technology more effectively, and because when technology benefits them in an exponential way, they become even more privileged.

Bridges.org states that digital divide is a comprehensive term and that access has to be evaluated and measured with respect to the following questions:

- Is technology available and physically accessible?
- What is the appropriate technology according to local conditions, and how do people want to put technology to use?

---

[66] See Pippa Norris, *Digital divide? Civic engagement, information poverty and the Internet world-wide* (Cambridge: Cambridge University Press, 2001).

[67] Bridges.org., *Spanning the digital divide: Understanding and tackling the issues: Executive summary*, 2004. Accessed 11 October 2010, at http://www.bridges.org/spanning/summary.html.

- Is access affordable for people?
- Do people understand how to use technology and its potential benefits?
- Is there locally relevant content, especially in terms of language?
- Does technology further burden people's lives or does it integrate into daily routines?
- Are people limited in their use of technology based on gender, race or other socio-cultural factors?
- Do people have confidence in and understand the implications of the technology they use; for instance in terms of privacy, security or cybercrime?
- How do laws and regulations affect technology use and what changes are needed to create an environment that fosters its use?
- Is there a local economy that can and will sustain technology use?
- Is national economic policy conducive to widespread technology use – for example, in terms of transparency, deregulation, investment and labour issues?
- Is there political will in government to do what is needed to enable the integration of technology into society?

Although the concept is often criticised as being simplistic and dichotomous, it reflects concerns about the lack of accessibility among vulnerable subpopulations such as the poor, the elderly and people with disabilities. Unfortunately, there is scant knowledge about the state of people with disabilities.[68] It is assumed that people with disabilities currently lack accessibility due to design, development and fabrication of telecommunications services and products. This exclusion becomes even more compelling as technologies converge and the pace of change increases when more products and services are made available through new means of digitisation. Generally, 'digital divides' for people with disabilities are evident in many areas: intellectual, visual and hearing abilities; changes due to ageing; differences in fine motor skills and abilities to purchase and receive access to emergency information.

---

[68] See arguments in *Closing the digital divide: Transforming regional economies and communities with information technology*. Edited by Stewart Marshall, Wallace Taylor and Xinghuo Yu (Westport, CT: Praeger, 2003).

CONCLUSION

This chapter demonstrated the link between historically depicted images of disability and how media culture constructs the current portrayals of disability. Printed and primarily digital media such as movies and TV shows play important roles in shaping public attitudes toward people with disabilities and the public's willingness to integrate them into social and civic society. Particular attention was given to the mixed influence of classical literature, children's TV programmes and the press, as well as Hollywood's role and advertising campaigns.

As a response to these influences, people with disabilities are often caught between the drive to form identities based on shared feelings of exclusion ('disability culture') and the feeling that their unique identities hamper their ability to integrate into society. A fascinating example that has already been discussed in depth is the Deaf culture and the threat of the cochlear implants to their identity.

Finally, people with disabilities lack accessibility in design, development and fabrication of telecommunications services and products. If society is interested in social inclusion, it needs to bridge the digital divide and to prevent it from turning into a social divide.

Part 2 **STRATEGIES TO PROMOTE SOCIAL INCLUSION**

5 SOCIAL STRATEGIES TO PROMOTE SOCIAL INCLUSION: SOCIAL PROTECTION AND SOCIAL CAPITAL

Article 28 of the CRPD[1] states the rights of people with disabilities to an adequate standard of living and social protection. The article includes the following:

1. States parties recognize the right of persons with disabilities to an adequate standard of living for themselves and their families, including adequate food, clothing and housing, and to the continuous improvement of living conditions, and shall take appropriate steps to safeguard and promote the realization of this right without discrimination on the basis of disability.

2. States parties recognize the right of persons with disabilities to social protection and to the enjoyment of that right without discrimination on the basis of disability, and shall take appropriate steps to safeguard and promote the realization of this right, including measures:

   (a) To ensure equal access by persons with disabilities to clean water services, and to ensure access to appropriate and affordable services, devices and other assistance for disability-related needs;

   (b) To ensure access by persons with disabilities, in particular women and girls with disabilities and older persons with disabilities, to social protection programs and poverty reduction programs;

   (c) To ensure access by persons with disabilities and their families living in situations of poverty to assistance from the State with

---

[1] UN Convention on the Rights of Persons with Disabilities: Article 28. Accessed 19 November 2011, http://www.un.org/disabilities/default.asp?id=288. The text was adopted by the United Nations General Assembly on 13 December 2006 and opened for signature on 30 March 2007. Following ratification by the twentieth party, it came into force on 3 May 2008. As of October 2011, it has 153 signatories and 106 parties.

disability-related expenses, including adequate training, counseling, financial assistance and respite care;
(d) To ensure access by persons with disabilities to public housing programs;
(e) To ensure equal access by persons with disabilities to retirement benefits and programs.

Article 28 identifies two basic provisions: (1) adequate standard of living and (2) social protection. This chapter will review and analyse social protection policies aimed at offering optimal social inclusion in different countries.

This chapter discusses two major strategies: social protection and social capital. The first strategy consists of labour market intervention, social insurance and social safety nets used in different Western countries. The second strategy, social capital, is used primarily in Europe to develop and sustain the inclusion of people with disabilities and families in community life.

SOCIAL PROTECTION POLICY AND SOCIAL INCLUSION OF PEOPLE WITH DISABILITIES

Social protection is defined as

> [T]he set of all initiatives, both formal and informal, that provide social assistance to extremely poor individuals and households; social services to groups who need special care or would otherwise be denied access to basic services; social insurance to protect people against the risks and consequences of livelihood of shocks; and social equity to protect people against social risks such as discrimination or abuse.[2]

Social protection intervention varies from humanitarian food assistance to employment and income-generation policies to create synergies with social inclusion measures.

---

[2] See Stephen Devereux and Rachel Sabates-Wheeler, IDS Working Paper 232, '*Transformative social protection*' (Brighton: Institute of Development Studies). Accessed 9 November 2011, www.ids.ac.uk/files/Wp232.pdf.

The practical use of the term is to describe interventions supporting the basic needs of vulnerable populations and individuals. The most recognised condition associated with social protection is chronic poverty. For that reason, typical social protection policies are redistributive in nature in order to offer feasible solutions for chronic poverty.[3]

Social protection policies are based on a wide array of public and community instruments that can be both contributive and non-contributive. These instruments include insurance, safety nets, cash and in-kind transfers, as well as labour-related protection. They are often classified according to their function, promotion and protection. *Promotion* refers to building up capabilities in the long term, while *protection* is a short-term policy that ensures provision of basic needs.

LABOUR MARKET INTERVENTIONS

In general, labour market interventions consist of both *active* and *passive* programmes that provide protection for people who are incapable of gaining employment. Typical passive programmes deal with maintenance – including unemployment insurance – income support and labour regulations aimed at alleviating the financial needs of the unemployed. Active programmes aim to reduce unemployment by improving access to the labour market. They are used to reduce the risk of unemployment by increasing the ability of the unemployed to find jobs and subsequently improving productivity and earnings. The expectation is that these interventions may enhance participation in productive employment. These programmes have the ability to increase employment opportunities and address the social problems that often accompany high unemployment rates. Active programmes are a way of reversing the negative effects of industrial restructuring in transition economies and to help integrate vulnerable populations that are farthest from the labour markets.

---

[3] See Samuel Hickey, CPRC Working Paper 151, 'The government of chronic poverty: From exclusion to citizenship?' (Manchester: University of Manchester, Institute for Development Policy and Management, Chronic Poverty Research Centre, 2010). Accessed 22 November 2011, http://www.chronicpoverty.org/publications/details/the-government-of-chronic-poverty-from-exclusion-to-citizenship.

There are a variety of protective and promotional tools that are often used at the national level to promote employment for people with disabilities and therefore reduce unemployment and underemployment.[4] *Regulations* are used in most of the countries to directly affect employers' hiring practices. Hiring quotas, which are accompanied by fines for noncompliant employers, are a traditional regulatory tool. A more recent tool is antidiscrimination legislation, which protects the rights of people with disabilities in the workplace and fines employers who refuse to make reasonable accommodations.

Quotas originated with hiring veterans with disabilities after World War I. The rationale then was compensatory, fulfilling the duty toward those who placed their lives in danger for their own countries. A few countries, including Germany, Austria, Italy and Poland established quota systems in the early 1920s.[5] After World War II, a second generation of quota policies was extended to veterans and then to civilian populations. By 2001, ten out of fourteen EU member states had various distinct forms of employment quota policies in operation. The countries without quotas included the UK and the Scandinavian countries Denmark, Finland and Sweden.[6] Employment quota policies have also been extensively used in the developing world. China, Cambodia, Thailand, Japan, Mongolia, India and Sri Lanka are among the countries using a range of quota or quota-style employment policies in their disability employment frameworks.

Quotas can be statutory or obligatory. The statutory quota requires the cooperation and compliance of employers. However, this type of quota

---

[4] See Daniel Mont, 'Disability employment policy', Social Protection Discussion Papers 30162 (Washington D.C.: The World Bank, 2004). Accessed 22 October 2011, http://ideas.repec. org/p/wbk/hdnspu/30162.html.

[5] Lisa Waddington and Matthew Diller, 'Tensions and coherence in disability policy: The uneasy relationship between social welfare and civil rights models of disability in American, European and international employment law', International Disability Law and Policy Symposium, 2000. Accessed 11 July 2008, http://www.dredf.org/international/waddington.html. The paper was published in 2002 in Mary Lou Breslin & Silvia Yee (Eds.), *Disability Rights Law and Policy, International and National Perspectives* (pp. 241–80). Transnational Publishers. The chapter analyzed also whether the disagreement between the civil rights model and the social welfare/medical model can be resolved.

[6] See Aoife Brennan and Pauline Conroy, 'The three percent target for the employment of people with disabilities in the public service (Dublin: National Disability Authority, 2004), Paper No 12, accessed 11 October 2011, http://www.nda.ie/cntmgmtnew.nsf/0/ E7AF211E4C77D7408025706600506DFE?OpenDocument.

was abandoned in the UK mainly because this tool did not produce satisfactory outcomes. Employers tended to be too selective and offered jobs to employees with mild disabilities while excluding those with severe disabilities.

The obligatory quota needs strong enforcement on the part of the State. This type of quota is often restricted to selected firms or highly functioning workers with disabilities. In some countries, such as Italy, a special nationwide quota hiring law applies to young persons with certain types of disabilities who complete vocational and technical training. In Israel, public companies are required to hire a quota of 5 percent veterans with disabilities, and there is a fine for those who fail to fill the quota.[7]

The Japanese employment policy is a quota-levy programme. Under this programme, employers are legally required to employ people with disabilities in proportion to their representation in the overall labour market. Levies are collected from enterprises failing to achieve the appropriate employment quota rate and grants are offered to enterprises that employ people with physical disabilities. While the quota-levy programme has traditionally been limited to people with physical disabilities, it now includes people with intellectual disabilities as well. Some employers prefer to pay the fine rather than going to the trouble of specially recruiting a very small number of workers. For example, in the Japanese private sector, more than half of the enterprises do not fulfil their quota obligations.

Counterbalances are policies that are designed to increase the competitiveness of people with disabilities in the labour market.[8] People with disabilities are often viewed as less skilled or less productive and are therefore seen as requiring more training and support than people without disabilities. The common tools used by counterbalance policies include wage subsidies, vocational rehabilitation and accommodation in the workplace.

Wage subsidy schemes are given to employers to reduce the extra cost of hiring people with disabilities, but also on the supply-side to increase the productivity and integration of employees with disabilities. They are

---

[7] Melvin Brodsky, 'Employment programs for disabled youth: An international view', *Monthly Labor Review* (1990) 113, 50–3. Accessed 10 October 2011, http://www.questia.com/googleScholar.qst;jsessionid=JLdTp429RywVLz5lKQk9kSKmQWD5t5FTwW2GGrTZc5FyNJ8p5XW4!349286206?docId=5000128277.

[8] See Mont, 'Disability employment policy', 27–8.

widely used in Australia, Sweden, Denmark, France, the Netherlands, Austria and Norway. Sweden and Japan are examples of countries that provide wage subsidies to compensate employers for the lower productivity related to disability.[9]

In Japan, the subsidy normally ranges from one-third to one-half of the wages paid and is usually limited to approximately eighteen months. Funds are also provided to employers for on-the-job training of disabled workers with the hope that after the training period the employer will continue their employment. Sweden uses differential wage subsidies: Public employers receive reimbursement of the total wage cost, whereas non-profit employers receive 90 percent and other employers receive 25 to 50 percent or, where relevant, 50 to 90 percent. The United States uses the Targeted Jobs Tax Credit programme to offer age support for workers with disabilities. Under this programme, tax credits are provided to employers against the first-year wages paid to newly hired workers from certain designated groups, including those with disabilities.

A literature review on wage subsidies for people with disabilities shows that they have mixed results.[10] Subsidies are expected to create job opportunities for some people who may not otherwise have that opportunity. They are also considered to be an incentive to employers to change their traditional hiring practices. However, subsidies are often viewed in the literature as a problematic instrument.[11] There is a concern that employment may not last beyond the subsidised period and that workers may be stigmatised if their employment is perceived as subsidised.

An interesting experience with German employers demonstrates that subsidies can cause windfall profits.[12] In this example, the majority of grants were given to a relatively small number of large firms. Analysis

[9] See Lawrence F. Katz, 'Wage subsidies for the disadvantaged'. In *Generating jobs: How to increase demand for less skilled workers*, Edited by Richard B. Freeman and Peter Gottschalk (New York: Russell Sage Foundation, 1998), pp. 21–53.

[10] John Mangan, 'Wage subsidies for the disabled: A discussion of their impact in Australia', *International Journal of Manpower* 11 (1990), 20–5.

[11] Gary Burtless, 'Are targeted wage subsidies harmful? Evidence from a wage voucher experiment', *Industrial & Labor Relations Review* 39 (1985), 105–14.

[12] Patricia Thornton and Neil Lunt, *Employment policies for disabled people in eighteen countries: A review* (Great Britain: York, Social Policy Research Unit/ ILO/ European Communities, 1997).

of the impact of the subsidies between 1976 and 1986 showed that 75 to 85 percent of the hiring would have taken place without a subsidy. Financial incentives for employers can also be offered in the form of tax deductions and tax credits rather than actual cash subsidies. This is extensively practised in the United States, Luxembourg, Poland and the Czech Republic.

A different approach to boosting employment of people with disabilities is to provide the incentive directly to people with disabilities rather than the employers. An interesting example occurred recently in Israel. Judge Laron Committee offered a recommendation to reform disability benefits paid by the National Insurance Institute.[13] It found that people with disabilities receiving disability benefits had a disincentive to work because they might face a reduction of their disability allowance and associated benefits. In order to boost integration into the labour market, the committee recommended a gradual reduction in payment of the allowance so that the total income of the beneficiary would increase. The new amendment intended to remove any obstacle to integration into the labour market and mandated, inter alia, that the total income derived from work and benefits of a person with disabilities would be higher than the income from the allowance alone.[14] It is too early to assess the policy, but the expectation is that it will increase the number of people with disabilities who will consider employment. However, the report has been criticised by academics and disability advocates as simplistic and inadequate because it assumes that the only obstacle to obtaining a job is insufficient incentives available to people with disabilities and lack of labour market supply.[15]

Do wage subsidies address the unemployment consequences of weak growth? A temporary wage subsidy does not necessarily induce sustained

---

[13] Judge Laron's report was released on 21 April 2005. There is only a Hebrew version, which can be accessed from http://www.pmo.gov.il/PMO/Archive/Events/2005/04/eventLaron210405.htm.

[14] The National Insurance Law (Amendment no. 109) (Promotion of the Integration of People with Disabilities into the Labor Market), 2007, became effective on 1 August 2009.

[15] See Kobi Cohen, 'The Laron report: Why is it important to stop implementation?'. Accessed 4 January 2011, http://mate.ios.st/IOS/Users/mate.ios.st/Files/3546613314.pdf (Hebrew).

growth in employment demand. It is conceivable – and many proponents of wage subsidies make this case – that workers gain experience and skills during their period of subsidised employment. The policy has been viewed by disability advocates as compensating employers for the loss of productivity of people with disabilities and sends a message that people with disabilities are inferior.[16]

The United States is a pioneer in vocational rehabilitation (VR) programmes.[17] A typical VR programme includes diagnostic evaluation, medical restoration, job placement and training. Numerous experimental studies of the efficacy of vocational rehabilitation have been reported in the research literature. Meta-analysis investigations have concluded that clients benefit considerably from various types of psychotherapeutic and counselling interventions.[18] Another recta-analysis of 475 controlled outcome studies, demonstrated an average effect size of .85 standard deviation on the outcome measure of the treatment over the control group, indicating that the typical client receiving vocational rehabilitation counselling was better off than 80 percent of those untreated and in need of counselling.[19]

In terms of cost effectiveness, one of the central studies that have examined the cost effectiveness of the federal-state VR programme found that VR returns roughly $2.50 USD for each dollar spent. The Rehabilitation Service Administration (RSA), which administers the federal-state VR programme, reported to Congress that every dollar spent on VR to return people with disabilities to gainful employment generates $18.00 in tax revenue to the government.[20]

Another popular strategy is *supported employment*, geared to help people with disabilities participate as much as possible in the competitive

---

[16] See, for example, Mangan, 'Wage subsidies for the disabled', 20–5.

[17] See, for example, Esco C. Obermann, *A history of vocational rehabilitation in America* (New York: Arno Press, 1980).

[18] See Mary L. Smith and Gene V. Glass, 'Meta-analysis of psychotherapy outcome studies', *American Psychologist* 32 (1977), 752–60; and Bruce E. Wampold, *The great psychotherapy debate: Models, methods, and findings* (Mahwah, NJ: Erlbaum, 2001).

[19] Steven R. Pruett et al. 'Empirical evidence supporting the effectiveness of vocational rehabilitation', *Journal of Rehabilitation*, 74 (2008), 53–63.

[20] David H. Dean, Robert C. Dolan and Robert M. Schmidt, 'Evaluating the vocational rehabilitation program using longitudinal data: Evidence for a quasi-experimental research design', *Evaluation Review* 23 (1999), 162–189.

labour market.[21] It was established in the early 1980s as a federal initiative to improve the quality of life of persons with severe disabilities.[22] Supported employment provides assistance to individuals with severe handicaps who are not able to function in competitive employment without ongoing support, which includes the provision of periodic or continuous services which may be provided both on the job (e.g., job coaching, paid co-workers, job modifications and adaptations) and outside of work (e.g., transportation and mobility instruction, time and money management). The underlying assumption is that individuals should be provided with as much assistance as needed for as long as needed to maintain employment.

State agency responsibility for supported employment services was limited to eighteen months.[23] States were given the responsibility of establishing interagency agreements in order to ensure the provision of long-term support services after the eighteen-month period had expired. Moreover, states such as New York determined that individuals should be transferred to extended services when they required less than 20 percent on-site support per week for three consecutive weeks. Such a transfer could occur before the eighteen-month period has expired.

Since its creation in the 1980s, supported employment has been studied extensively. The primary question is whether these programmes are effective and can be justified as such to taxpayers. Early research explored the cost efficiency or cost effectiveness of supported employment programmes.[24] For the most part, supported employment was proven to be a good investment for taxpayers;[25] that is, for every dollar that taxpayers put into supported employment programmes, they received more than a dollar back in the form of monetary benefits.

---

[21] Gary R. Bond, Deborah R. Becker, Robert E. Drake, Charles A. Rapp, Neil Meisler, Anthony F. Lehman, Morris Bell, and Crystal R. Blyler, 'Implementing supported employment as an evidence-based practice', *Psychiatric Services* 52 (2001), 313–22.

[22] See Madeleine Will, 'Supported employment', Washington, D.C., U.S., an OSERS position paper, 1984, and Jean K. Elder, 'Job opportunities for developmentally disabled people', *American Rehabilitation* 10 (1984), 26–30.

[23] Federal Register (14 August 1987) 52(157), 30546–30552. 34 CFR 363; (14 August 1987), 52(157), 30546–30552. 34 CFR 363.

[24] Robert E. Cimera, 'The cost-effectiveness of supported employment and sheltered workshops in Wisconsin: FY 2002–2005', *Journal of Vocational Rehabilitation* 26 (2007), 153–8.

[25] Robert E. Cimera, 'The monetary costs and benefits of hiring supported employees: Revisited', *Journal of Vocational Rehabilitation*, 24 (2006), 137–44.

Recent research that studied the cost efficiency of all 231,204 people with intellectual disabilities as supported employees between 2002 and 2007 found that they returned an average monthly net benefit to taxpayers of $251.34 (i.e., an annual net benefit of $3,016.08 per supported employee) and generated a benefit-cost ratio of 1.46. Even individuals with the least cost-efficient disability (i.e., traumatic brain injuries) returned a monthly net benefit of $111.62 to taxpayers.[26]

Workplace accommodations comprise another strategy aimed at removing barriers in the workplace for people with disabilities in order to achieve full integration into the workplace.[27] Workplace accommodations interventions involve changes to the work environment that are typically practice-related, technological or environmental in nature. The assumption is that employers lack information on available assistive technology options. The belief is that universally designed devices provide great benefits for workers with disabilities because they allow them to integrate more easily into the environment with less need for changes to be implemented by employers.

In the United States, the right to be provided reasonable accommodations in the workplace is part of the amendments to the ADA, which is designed to remove barriers to employment for workers with disabilities. Under the ADA, accommodations begin in the hiring process. Employers must make *reasonable accommodations* for applicants who are qualified for the job for which they are applying. Accommodations may include providing a sign language interpreter for a deaf applicant or ensuring that the interview is held in a wheelchair-accessible building for a paraplegic applicant. Once hired, workers with disabilities are entitled to all the benefits and privileges of employment. Employers may need to adjust training, provide or modify equipment or ensure that disabled workers have equal access to information communicated to non-disabled workers.

---

[26] Robert E. Cimera, 'National cost efficiency of supported employees with intellectual disabilities: 2002 to 2007', *American Journal of Intellectual and Developmental Disabilities* 115 (2010), 119–29.

[27] See, for example, Carrie Bruce and Jon A. Sanford, 'Assessment for workplace accommodation'. In *Assessment in rehabilitation and health*. Edited by Thomas Oakland and Elias Mpofu (Upper Saddle, NJ: Prentice Hall, 2009); and Jon A. Sanford and Karen Milchus, 'Evidence-based practice in workplace accommodations', *Work* 27 (2006), 329–32.

It is evident that the ADA has increased not only employers' attention to job accommodations but also their concerns regarding the cost of providing accommodations for current and potential employees with disabilities. A study that examined the influence of workplace accommodations on the labour market found that accommodations have a positive effect on job tenure.[28] Because accommodations are costly to firms, it is likely that a concern may be passed on to workers with disabilities in the form of a reduced wage.[29] Unfortunately, only 12 percent of people with disabilities in the workplace enjoy workplace accommodations.[30] Accommodations were primarily used by full-time employees that were educated females with disabilities. Provisions were also greater for more severe limitations, but were less likely for those with mental health impairments.

A recent study conducted by the Job Accommodation Network (JAN) showed that the benefits employers receive from making workplace accommodations far outweigh the costs.[31] Employers reported that providing accommodations resulted in benefits such as retaining valuable employees, improving productivity and morale, reducing workers' compensation and training costs, and improving company diversity.

These benefits were also obtained with little investment. The employers in the study reported that a high percentage (56 percent) of accommodations cost absolutely nothing to provide, whereas the remaining percentage typically cost only $600. Similar findings were reported in another recent study, suggesting that the costs of accommodating employees with disabilities are minimal, with a change in work schedule being the most common request.[32]

[28] Richard V. Burkhauser, J. S. Butler and Yang woo Kim, 'The importance of employer accommodation on the job duration of workers with disabilities: A hazard model approach', *Later Economics* 2 (1995), 109–30.

[29] Marjorie L. Baldwin and William G. Johnson, 'Labor market discrimination against men with disabilities in the year of the ADA', *Southern Economic Journal* 66 (2000), 548–66.

[30] Craig Zwerling et al., 'Workplace accommodations for people with disabilities: National health interview survey disability supplement, 1994–1995', *Journal of Occupation and Environmental Medicine* 45 (2003), 517–25.

[31] Job Accommodation Network, 'Workplace accommodations: Low cost, high impact'. Accessed 18 January 2010, www.jan.wvu.edu/media/LowCostHighImpact.doc.

[32] Brigida Hernandez and Katherine McDonald, 'Exploring the costs and benefits of workers with disabilities', *Journal of Rehabilitation* 76 (2010), 15–23.

Similar to the United States, the most significant progress in workplace accommodations for people with disabilities in the UK was a result of disability discrimination legislation.[33] The most important part of the law against disability discrimination is the obligation of employers to make reasonable adjustments. Basically, employers must take reasonable steps to adjust hours or duties, buy or modify equipment or allow time off so that workers can carry out their jobs.

However, employer compliance in the UK was related to the cost of job adjustment. The cost of making adjustments was the major concern to small employers and service providers. A similar survey reported that UK contractors were more likely to make 'reasonable adjustments' as required by the UK DDA if the adjustment was relatively inexpensive and if minimal adjustments were required in order to adapt workplaces in such a way to provide an inclusive approach to the employment of disabled people.[34]

The use of regulations implies that people with disabilities are capable of participating in the labour market and that the modest cost of their integration can be easily absorbed by private corporations and enterprises. Counterbalances are used if the assumption is that people with disabilities cannot participate in the workforce without wage subsidies, vocational rehabilitation or training. The expectation is that the cost of these interventions has to be paid by the general public and not by private employers.

Substitutions are different in nature; they are used in cases where people with disabilities cannot be integrated into the free labour market. Sheltered employment is the most prevalent model of substitution for competitive employment.[35] The term is often used to describe a wide range of segregated vocational and non-vocational programmes for individuals with disabilities such as sheltered workshops, adult activity

---

[33] The Disability Discrimination Act (DDA) of 1995 was an Act of Parliament of the United Kingdom that stated that it is unlawful to discriminate against people in respect of their disabilities in relation to employment, the provision of goods and services, education and transport. The DDA was repealed and replaced by the Equality Act of 2010.

[34] Marcus G. Ormerod and Rita A. Newton, 'Moving beyond accessibility: The principles of universal (inclusive) design as a dimension in nD modeling of the built environment', *Architectural Engineering and Design Management* 1 (2005), 103–10.

[35] Laurent Visier, 'Sheltered employment for persons with disabilities', *International Labor Review*, 137 (1998), 347–65.

centres, work activity centres and day treatment centres. These programmes differ extensively in terms of their mission, services provided and funding sources. Currently, most sheltered employment services are operated through private not-for-profit organisations that are funded through a variety of state and federal funding sources.

There are two types of sheltered employment programmes in the United States.[36] The first, *transitional* employment programmes, aims to provide training and experience to individuals in segregated settings so that they will be able to acquire the skills necessary to succeed in subsequent competitive employment. The second type, *extended* employment programmes, is designed to provide permanent placements for disabled individuals that will allow them to use their existing abilities to earn wages in the segregated workshop setting.

However, the two types of sheltered employment programmes attracted criticism from disability rights activists and the professional community. The general impression was that supported employment is a preferable alternative to sheltered employment.[37] The scepticism is related to the inability of sheltered employment programmes to prepare people for productive jobs and to the fact that these programmes are segregated in nature and encourage social exclusion of people with disabilities. These facilities are criticised for being inconsequential, paying low wages and increasing dependency on federal cash benefit programmes. In terms of social inclusion, sheltered employment facilities are often segregated and downgrade the image of people with disabilities as productive and equal members of the community.

Countries differ in their *substitutions* policies and sheltered employment programmes. Sheltered and extended employment programmes became less popular in the United States in the early 1980s. The federal government and the states preferred the development of supported employment programmes, which are based on integration in the

[36] John K. Kregel and David H. Dean, 'Sheltered vs. supported employment: A direct comparison of long-term earning outcomes for individuals with cognitive disabilities'. In *Achievements and challenges in employment services for people with disabilities: A longitudinal impact of workplace supports*. Edited by John Kregel et al., 2002. Accessed 11 December 2011, www.worksupport.com/main/downloads/dean/shelteredchap3.pdf.

[37] Jeanne Novak, Pat Rogan and Dale DiLeo, 'Supported employment and systems change: Findings from a national survey of state vocational rehabilitation agencies', *Journal of Vocational Rehabilitation* 19 (2003), 157–66.

workplace. European countries and South America have mixed systems of sheltered and supported employment.

Cost-benefit analyses completed in the United States during the 1990s indicated that integrated employment options such as supported employment significantly improved individuals' earnings and economic self-sufficiency.[38] They cost less than sheltered workshops and extended employment programmes and decreased dependency on disability benefits. However, in practice, the majority of individuals with severe intellectual disabilities attend sheltered and extended employment programmes. They are more popular among adults with moderate to severe intellectual disability. Parents are often concerned that integrated settings cannot offer their adult children the same safety, adequate transportation and stability as sheltered employment facilities.[39]

Similar practice was observed in Europe. A 1996 review of the policies of eighteen countries found that almost half of the fifteen EU member states preferred to expand the provision of sheltered employment.[40] Another report by the OECD revealed a similar trend toward policies favouring supported employment but offered no signs of a reduction in the number of people served in sheltered employment facilities.[41]

The debate about substitutions is also related to minimum wage policy. The common labour market regulation for underemployment and lack of opportunities to work and exposure to job skills is the Sub-minimum Wage (SMW),[42] which enables employers, under certain conditions, to pay persons with disabilities wages below the established minimum wage.[43]

---

[38] Cimera, 'National cost efficiency of supported employees with intellectual disabilities', 119–29.

[39] Alberto Migliore et al., 'Why do adults with intellectual disabilities work in sheltered workshops?' *Journal of Vocational Rehabilitation* 28 (2008), 29–40.

[40] Thornton and Lunt, *Employment policies for disabled people in eighteen countries*.

[41] See OECD, 'Transforming disability into ability: Policies to promote work and income security for disabled people' (2003), 113–4. Can be accessed from virk.is/static/files/4_disability%20to%20ability.pdf.

[42] John Butterworth et al., 'State and international efforts to reform or eliminate the use of sub-minimum wage for persons with disabilities' (Boston: Institute for Community Inclusion, University of Massachusetts, 2007).

[43] Michal Soffer, Patricia Tal-Katz and Arie Rimmerman, 'Sub minimum wage for persons with severe disabilities: Comparative perspectives', *Journal of Comparative Policy Analysis* 13 (2011), 265–86.

Supporters of SMW believe that it is an important tool to increase earnings of persons with severe disabilities and encourage their integration into competitive employment. Opponents of SMW see it as a regulated measure that does not significantly change the employment status of people with severe disabilities. Some suggest that sub-minimum wages may even be discriminatory and stigmatising.[44]

Comparison of SMW policies in the United States, Australia and Israel found that the three countries differ in terms of participants' participation in competitive versus non-competitive settings.[45] In the United States, SMW is used in sheltered industries; in Israel it is directed toward employment in competitive settings, while in Australia two separate programmes address both settings. In practice, in all countries' current participants in SMW are primarily persons with intellectual or psychiatric disabilities. Compared to Australia and Israel, the U.S. policy tends to minimise government regulation in the labour market, with the result that SMW is perceived as an exceptional solution, just for those working in sheltered industries. Australia and Israel tend to allow more government intervention and therefore imply that SMW is a valid policy to integrate people with severe disabilities into competitive employment settings.

These ideological and economic differences in government regulation are also evident in service delivery systems. In the United States the certified employer is the initiator of the process and is also the assessor and the one who determines the sub-minimum wage. Australia has a similar initiator (the employer or an employment service provider), but professionals from the allied health professions conduct the assessments and determinations of sub-minimum wages. The Israeli system marginalises the employer's role, thus the initiator is the person with disabilities, and the assessment and the determination of the sub-minimum wage is carried out by a professional outsourcing agency.

The different approaches toward SMW are observed in the way wages are calculated. In the United States, SMW is a direct percentage of the person's productivity rate (starting from 1 percent); in Australia it is the same (although starting from 10 percent) or a result of a fixed formula,

[44] Ibid.
[45] Ibid.

while in Israel it is a six-level ranking, starting from 30 percent of the minimum wage.[46]

A closer look at the findings, however, reveals that the documented differences are misleading. While they are probably products of different cultural, economic and political systems, they are merely variants of the same mechanism. It seems that in general the United States employer operates in a less-regulated economy. As shown earlier, Australia and Israel allow more government regulations and procedures aimed to protect the employment status of people with severe disabilities.

SOCIAL INSURANCE

Social insurance schemes are contributory programmes protecting beneficiaries from unexpected catastrophic expenses in exchange for regular payments of premiums. As such, they provide income support in the event of illness, disability, work injury, maternity, unemployment and old age. The list of programmes include: unemployment insurance to deal with frictional or structural unemployment; work injury insurance to compensate workers for work-related injuries or diseases; disability and invalidity insurance, normally linked to old-age pensions to cover full or partial disability; sickness and health insurance to protect workers from diseases; maternity insurance to provide benefits to mothers during pregnancy and post-delivery lactating months; old-age insurance to provide income support after retirement; and life and survivors' insurance, normally linked to the old-age pension, to ensure that dependents are compensated for the loss of a breadwinner.

The number of recipients of social security disability insurance (SSDI) in the United States has risen significantly since 1984.[47] A significant proportion of the rise in SSDI rolls has been attributed to the Social Security Disability Benefits Reform Act.[48] The study of changes in SSDI

---

[46] Ibid.

[47] Perry Singleton, 'The effective target of the Social Security Disability Benefits Reform Act of 1984', Syracuse University, Department of Economics, Center for Policy Research Working Paper No. 119 (Syracuse, NY: Syracuse University, 2009), pp. 23–4.

[48] The Social Security Disability Benefits Reform Act of 1984 (Public Law 98–460) was enacted in response to problems that arose as a result of the implementation by the Social Security Administration (SSA) of a provision in the 1980 disability amendments

benefits as related to labour supply has been confirmed in previous reports.[49] There has been a simultaneous increase in labour force participation and non-participation and receipt of SSDI. This suggests that SSDI benefits have substantial effects on labour supply behaviour. However, these findings can be misleading because those who are induced out of the labour market by SSDI benefits may not otherwise work.[50] Similar findings were reported in an early study indicating that those who removed themselves from the labour market did suffer from work limitations.[51]

Social assistance, provided as cash or in-kind transfers, is a core social protection tool used by governments as a poverty-reduction policy.[52] In recent years, there has been a debate about the merit of social assistance policies for vulnerable populations. Countries in Latin America, Africa and Asia tend to use them as the main tool to improve income security and nutrition, as well as health and access to education.[53] Those who oppose extensive use of social assistance programmes believe that they increase dependency and an inclination to become permanently dependent on them. There are also paternalistic and stereotypic arguments that poor people who are given social assistance will inevitably use the benefits inappropriately for gambling or obtaining alcohol instead of for their well-being.

that required periodic Continuing Disability Review (CDR). In enacting the new law, Congress intended to assure more accurate, consistent and uniform disability decisions at all levels, and equitable and humane treatment not only to beneficiaries who must undergo Continuing Disability Review but also to new applicants for Disability Insurance (DI) benefits or Supplemental Security Income (SSI) payments based on disability or blindness.

[49] See, for example, Donald Parsons, 'The decline in male labor force participation', *Journal of Political Economy* 88 (1980), 117–34.

[50] John Bound and Richard Burkhauser, 'Economic analysis of transfer programs targeted on people with disabilities'. In *Handbook of labor economics*, vol. 3. Edited by Orley Ashenfelter and David Card (Oxford: Elsevier Press, 1999), pp. 3417–528.

[51] John Bound and Timothy Waidman, 'Disability transfers, self-reported health, and the labor force attachment of older men: Evidence from the historical record', *Quarterly Journal of Economics* 107 (2002), 1393–419.

[52] Anna Marriott and Kate Gooding, *Social assistance and disability in developing countries: Reaching the disabled with social assistance programmes* (Haywards Heath, UK: Sightsavers International, 2007).

[53] See, for example, Stephen Devereux and Larissa Pelham, *Making cash count: Lessons from cash transfer schemes in east and southern Africa for supporting the most vulnerable children and households* (Brighton: University of Sussex, Save the Children UK, London, Help Age International, and IDS, 2005).

There is a distinction between in-kind transfers and cash transfers as tools. The latter was proven for promoting livelihoods via investments in micro-enterprises and the maintenance of productive assets.[54] Those who oppose in-kind transfers believe that they tend to reinforce dependency and that cash transfers inject capital into local markets and give recipients the dignity and empowerment of choice.[55]

People with disabilities are often identified as potential beneficiaries of social assistance programmes. They are vulnerable, often coping with tremendous crises that may leave them without adequate resources. Unfortunately, there is very little information about the use of social assistance in the United States, Europe and developing countries. This lack of information is related to the range of disabilities and the fact that different social, financial and physical environments create very different situations.[56] Furthermore, in many countries people who receive disability benefits and services are prevented from using social assistance.

The main justification for paying disability benefits is the close link between disability and poverty. It is evident that disability increases vulnerability to poverty, whereas poverty creates the conditions for increased risk of becoming disabled.[57] Widely quoted UN statistics suggest that one in five of the world's poorest people have a disability, and 82 percent of people with disabilities in developing countries live below the poverty line.[58]

Most of the research on social assistance is anecdotal and limited to developing countries.[59] A fairly comprehensive review of the literature

[54] See for example, Armando Barrientos and Peter Lloyd-Sherlock, *Non-contributory pensions and social protection*, Issues in Social Protection Series, Social Protection Sector (Geneva: International Labor Organisation, 2002).

[55] John Farrington and Rachel Slater, 'Introduction: Cash transfers: Panacea for poverty reduction or money down the drain?' *Development Policy Review* 24 (2006), 499–511.

[56] Teresa Guthrie and Wassheila Sait, *Social security policy options for people with disabilities in South Africa: An international and comparative view* (South Africa: Child Health Policy Institute and the South African Federal Council on Disability for the Committee of Inquiry into a Comprehensive Social Security System, 2001).

[57] Tony Emmett, 'Disability, poverty, gender and race'. In *Disability and social change: A South African agenda*. Edited by Brian Watermeyer et al. (South Africa: Human Sciences Research Council, 2006), p. 209.

[58] European Commission, *Guidance note on disability and development for EU delegations and services* (Brussels: DG Development, 2003).

[59] Marriott and Gooding, *Social assistance and disability in developing countries*.

confirms that individuals and households affected by disability are more likely to be below the poverty line and that being disabled increases the risk of becoming poor.[60] There are indications that social assistance may enable a contribution to the household budget and encourage mobilisation of people with disabilities. However, evidence on the economic status of the individuals with disabilities is less clear, particularly regarding employment. There are also reports that people with disabilities often lack control over spending of the grants. There is evidence that social assistance can improve access to health services, but the picture regarding education is more mixed, with access depending on provision of adequate services.

There are indications that governments do see social assistance as one option within a wider framework of support for education, employment and other rights, but there seems to be little integration among social assistance and these other measures. Unfortunately, policy makers still dichotomise people with disabilities between those with the potential for employment and productivity and the 'unfortunate' in need of social assistance. Updated policies have to balance social assistance with other measures, and policy makers need to consider an appropriate sequence of measures and the role of social assistance in compensating for the extra costs associated with disability. Possible strategies to improve integration include a more comprehensive assessment for disabled individuals that considers a range of needs and a clearer understanding of social assistance as a means rather than an end.

SOCIAL CAPITAL POLICIES TOWARD PEOPLE WITH DISABILITIES

Social capital was previously reviewed in relation to social exclusion. The term is used to explain networks of personal relationships (micro) and a wide range of social phenomena (macro), including community practices and economic performances. Social capital can be approached from different angles. According to Robert Putnam (1993), the most important theorist within the social capital paradigm, social capital is

---

[60] Kate Gooding, *Poverty and blindness: A survey of the literature* (Haywards Heath, UK: Sightsavers International, 2006).

'trust, norms, and networks, which can improve the efficiency of society by facilitating coordinated actions'.[61]

Social capital includes networking, personal trust and civic norms. It is often criticised as a loose term used primarily in community studies by activists and policy makers. Despite the above criticism, social capital is consonant with promotion of community coalescence, economic growth and prosperity. The term has been interpreted recently also with respect to the online community.[62]

SOCIAL CAPITAL AND THE EMPLOYMENT OF PEOPLE WITH DISABILITIES

Surprisingly, there is little research on social capital and employment of persons with disabilities. People with disabilities seem to have used their immediate social supports, primarily family members or relatives, to find a job.[63] Being excluded from community life, they are often detached from accessing information and resources, including potential employment contacts. In other words, people with disabilities do not use social capital as a potential asset for job placement or face significant barriers to utilising social capital in their career development.

Social capital can raise awareness among people with disabilities regarding job opportunities, receiving tips about access and different supports available including transportation and childcare.[64] Potts lists suggestions and tips that people receive from others in the network such as a valuable source of information about the 'hidden job market, or a friendly employer that may hire people with disabilities through personal ties'.[65]

---

[61] Robert D. Putnam, *Making democracy work: Civic traditions in modern Italy* (Princeton: Princeton University Press, 1993), p. 167.

[62] See, for example, Sarah Cummings, Richard Heeks, and Marleen Huysman, 'Knowledge and learning on online communities in development: A social capital perspective. Manchester: University of Manchester, Institute of Development Policy and Management. Working Paper 16, 2003. Accessed 8 January 2011 http://www.sed.manchester.ac.uk/idpm/research/publications/wp/di/di_wp16.htm.

[63] See, for example, David Hagner, John Butterworth and Geraldine Keith, 'Strategies and barriers in facilitating natural supports for employment of adults with severe disabilities', *Journal of the Association for Persons with Severe Handicaps* 20 (1995), 110–20.

[64] See Robert D. Putnam, *Dynamics of social capital* (Oxford: Oxford University Press, 2002).

[65] Blyden Potts, 'Disability and employment: Considering the importance of social capital', *Journal of Rehabilitation* 71 (2005), 20–5.

Research has demonstrated that job contact networks are hardly accessible to applicants with serious speech problems who use augmentative and alternative communication technology.[66] Similar experiences have been shared by adults with cerebral palsy who participated in a focus group related to their career development in their search for employment.[67] Those who have social capital can socialise occasionally outside the home in bars or in social clubs. They could also use their social network (social capital) with other co-workers to solve problems on the job.[68]

Unfortunately, people with disabilities are at a disadvantage with respect to their job networks compared to people without disabilities. If people with disabilities have higher unemployment rates compared to those without disabilities, they probably have less access to social capital and vice versa. There is linkage between the two and it is clear that the effort has to be in both directions.

The linkage between employment and social capital is applicable to employment specialists and vocational rehabilitation counsellors. They to need recognise the importance of social capital in finding jobs, what makes social networks more effective at finding jobs and how to help people build their social networks.

SOCIAL CAPITAL AND THE ONLINE COMMUNITY

The Web is a fairly new arena where people with and without disabilities can create online communities. Today it is assumed that online involvement is one of the ways to overcome difficulties in interpersonal relationships.[69] The rapid growth of cyberspace can facilitate the

---

[66] Allison Carey et al., 'Networking towards employment: Experiences of people who use augmentative and alternative communication', *Research and Practice for Persons with Severe Disabilities*, 29 (2004), 40–52.

[67] David McNaughton, Janice Light and Kara Arnold, 'Getting your 'wheel' in the door: Successful full-time employment experiences of individuals with cerebral palsy who use augmentative and alternative communication', *Augmentative and Alternative Communication* 18 (2002), 59–76.

[68] See Archie W. N. Roy, Gisela Dimigen and Marcella Taylor, 'The relationship between social networks and employment of visually impaired college graduates', *Journal of Visual Impairment and Blindness* 92 (1998), 423–32.

[69] Robert Kraut et al., 'Internet paradox: A social technology that reduces social involvement and psychological well-being?' *American Psychologist* 53 (1998), 1017–31.

construction and development of social capital in many ways. The Internet has great potential for building social capital and trust because it does not discriminate between people with and without disabilities.[70]

There are three components that have played an important role in this development: (1) the structure of online networks, (2) the flow of information in networks and (3) the formation of human relationships within these networks, with the latter clearly being the most important outcome of social capital online. This is possible in a huge country such as China where people with disabilities have demonstrated their success in creating social capital through the Internet.[71]

CONCLUSION

Social protection is a central and well-documented strategy in ensuring the economic necessities for self-sufficiency for those who are vulnerable or in distress. People with disabilities are frequent users of social protection provisions, which are usually delivered by labour market intervention, social insurance and social safety programmes. Although these interventions are common and widely used, there are concerns that they may perpetuate dependency and segregation, in particular, in terms of social security, social assistance and sheltered employment programmes.

A newer strategy is social capital, interpreted as networks of personal relationships and a wide range of social phenomena including community practices and economic performances. Social capital, used primarily in Europe, can serve as a core asset in finding and maintaining employment and in social and civic participation and social inclusion. However, while online networking is an asset for expanding social capital, unfortunately, people with disabilities are disadvantaged with respect to their employment and social and civic networks, compared to people without disabilities.

---

[70] John C. Pierce et al., 'Internet technology transfer and social capital: Aggregate and individual relationships in American cities', *Comparative Technology Transfer and Society* 1 (2003), 47–70.

[71] Howard Karger and Steven R. Rose, 'Revisiting the Americans with Disabilities Act after two decades', *Journal of Social Work in Disability & Rehabilitation*, 9: 73–86, 2010. Accessed 13 August 2011, http://www.tandfonline.com/doi/pdf/10.1080/1536710X.2010.493468.

6 NATIONAL DISABILITY RIGHTS: INSTRUMENTS AND MEASURES TO PROMOTE SOCIAL INCLUSION

Can disability rights legislation promote social inclusion of people with disabilities? In order to examine this important question this chapter reviews, analyses and compares national laws and measures that promote inclusive participation, among them the ADA of 1990/2008, the UK DDA of 1995/2005 and the Equality Act of 2010 and Israel's 1998 Equal Rights for Persons with Disabilities Law.

THE AMERICANS WITH DISABILITIES ACT OF 1990/2008

The Americans with Disabilities Act (ADA) signed by President George H. W. Bush in 1990 is the most comprehensive disability rights legislation in the United States. President Bush described it as a 'historic new civil rights Act.... the world's first comprehensive declaration of equality for people with disabilities'.[1] Others called it 'a watershed in the history of disability rights . . . the most far-reaching legislation ever enacted against discrimination of people with disabilities'.[2] A substantial body of disability law including the Rehabilitation Act of 1973,[3] the Education for All Handicapped Children Act of 1975,[4] the Fair Housing Amendments Act

---

[1] Remarks of President George H. W. Bush at the signing of the Americans with Disabilities Act. Accessed 1 October 2011, http://www.eeoc.gov/eeoc/history/35th/videos/ada_signing_text. html.

[2] The Congressional Office of Technology Assessment, U.S. Congress, Office of Technology Assessment, 1994.

[3] Public Law 93–112 93rd Congress, H. R. 8070 26 September 1973.

[4] The Education for All Handicapped Children Act (sometimes referred to by the acronyms EAHCA or EHA, or Public Law 94–142) was enacted by the U.S. Congress in 1975.

of 1988[5] and numerous state antidiscrimination disability statutes were already in place, but the ADA marked a dramatic change in the position of people with disabilities in American society. It is broader in scope than existing federal laws and prohibits discrimination not only in employment and public programmes but also in public accommodations. The ADA covers all employers and service providers, not just public and publicly funded ones. The legislation emerged from Congress with bipartisan support, promising equality of opportunity, full participation, independent living and economic self-sufficiency for people with disabilities. Its intention is comprehensive, as stated: 'not just persons with disabilities and persons charged with respecting and enforcing human rights, but virtually every segment of our society – *all* Americans' (emphasis added).[6]

The law extends similar civil rights to people with disabilities that other groups already have on the basis of race, sex, national origin and religion. The ADA prohibits discrimination on the basis of disability in employment, in state and local government activities and in public accommodations and services, including transportation. The 1990 legislation includes five titles, which are discussed in the following sections.

TITLE I. EMPLOYMENT

This prohibits discrimination against qualified individuals with disabilities with regards to employment. The act provides individuals with protection from discriminatory treatment arising from corporate activities and policies governing recruitment, hiring, training, promotion, pay, job assignment, leaves of absence, benefits and social programmes. For employers with twenty-five or more employees, the requirements became effective on 26 July 1992. For employers with fifteen to twenty-four employees, the requirements became effective on 26 July 1994.

---

[5] Congress passed the Fair Housing Amendments Act on 13 September 1988, extending coverage of Title VIII of the Civil Rights Act of 1968 (the Fair Housing Act) to prohibit discriminatory housing practices based on disability and family status. The Fair Housing Act also prohibits discrimination in the sale, rental and financing of dwellings based on race, color, religion, sex and national origin.

[6] Lawrence O. Gostin and Harry A. Beyer, 'Preface'. In *Implementing the Americans with Disabilities Act: Rights and responsibilities of all Americans*. Edited by Lawrence O. Gostin and Harry A. Beyer (Baltimore: Brookes Publishing, 1993), p. xiii.

TITLE II. PUBLIC SERVICES

This prohibits discrimination in programmes, services or activities of public entities (state and local governments), including public transportation operated by public entities. The provisions of Title II that did not involve public transportation became effective on 26 January 1992.

TITLE III. PUBLIC ACCOMMODATIONS AND COMMERCIAL FACILITIES

This title requires that private businesses that are open to the public – including restaurants, department stores, convenience stores, specialty shops, hotels and motels – allow individuals with disabilities to participate equally in the goods and services offered. This title also requires that all future commercial facilities, including office buildings, factories and warehouses, as well as places of public accommodation, be constructed so that they are accessible to individuals with disabilities. Title III also mandates modifications in policies, practices and procedures; the provision of auxiliary aids and services; the provision of accessible transportation services when transportation services are offered; and the removal of architectural and communications barriers.

TITLE IV. TELECOMMUNICATIONS

This title requires telephone companies to make relay services available for persons with hearing and speech impairments. This provides equal opportunities to people with speech or hearing impairments to use telephone services. The requirements became effective on 26 July 1993.

TITLE V. MISCELLANEOUS

This title ties the ADA to the Civil Rights Act of 1964 and its subsequent amendments. It includes a variety of legal and technical provisions, including a provision that stipulates that the ADA does not override or limit the remedies, rights or procedures of any federal, state or local law that provides equal or greater protection for the rights of individuals with disabilities.

A few of the key terms and definitions in the ADA are 'Public Accommodation', 'Reasonable Accommodations' and 'Readily Achievable'. As defined in the ADA, the term *Public Accommodations* refers to any private place of business that is open to the public for the sale or lease of goods and services. The act lists twelve general categories of public accommodation:

1. Places of lodging
2. Places serving food or drink
3. Places of exhibition and/or entertainment
4. Places of public gathering
5. Sales or rental establishments
6. Service establishments
7. Stations used for specified public transportation
8. Places of public display or collection
9. Places of recreation
10. Places of education
11. Social service centre establishments
12. Places of exercise or recreation

There are two types of actions that employers or public places are required to undertake for people with disabilities: *Reasonable Accommodations* and *Readily Achievable*. *Reasonable Accommodations* is related to qualified employees or applicants for employment. The accommodations have to be reasonable in terms of cost imposed on employers. *Readily Achievable* is associated with clients or guests in terms of how easy it is to carry out actions without much difficulty or expense. Readily achievable modifications must be made in anticipation of a client or guest with a disability before they arrive on the premises.

The ADA is civil rights legislation similar to protections offered by the federal government for women and racial, ethnic and religious minorities. Therefore, the ADA raised high expectations in addressing the barriers to participation by people with disabilities in the mainstream of society.[7] Jane West believed that 'the greatest impact of the ADA to date is in two areas:

[7] Karger and Rose, 'Revisiting the Americans with Disabilities Act after two decades', p. 83.

the empowerment claimed by people with disabilities and changes in how our nation's institutions conduct routine business: in stores, on buses, in the office, and in our use of telecommunications'.[8] Self-perception and the accessibility of everyday life are interrelated and are central concepts in this civil rights law.

The ADA has significantly changed how society views and accommodates its citizens with disabilities. The concept of universal design has changed the practice of designing products, buildings, and public spaces and programmes to be usable by the greatest number of people. There is no doubt that the ADA has created a more inclusive society and has encouraged companies, institutions and organisations to enhance the level of participation of people with disabilities.

The United States became the first country to adopt national civil rights legislation, banning discrimination against people with disabilities in the public and private sectors. The ADA is a pioneering legislation, supported by disability organisations, bipartisan members of the House of Representatives and the Senate, the business community and civil society. Judith Heumann, an internationally well-known disability activist,[9] believes that the ADA has had a profound impact both in the United States and abroad. Domestically, the ADA, in tandem with other disability legislation, has contributed to better inclusion of people with disabilities in all areas of life. This success at home has encouraged many other nations to abandon traditional welfare approaches and adopt this progressive non-discrimination legislation as disability rights practice. The ADA is often viewed as one of the inspirations for the CRPD.

However, the ADA has been criticised for being disappointing with respect to labour market practices.[10] Employment levels among people

---

[8] Jane West, 'Introduction'. In *Implementing the Americans with Disabilities Act*. Edited by Jane West (Cambridge, MA: Blackwell Publishers and Millbank Memorial Fund, 1996), note 6 at p. xiv.

[9] She participated as a blogger. Accessed 7 November 2011, http://blog.govdelivery.com/usodep/2011/07/celebrating-the-americans-with-disabilities-act-ada-at-home-and-abroad.html.

[10] See Ruth Colker, *The Americans with Disabilities Act: A windfall for defendants*, 34 HARV. C.R.-C.L. L. REV. 99, 100 (1999), discussing that defendants prevail in more than 93 percent of reported ADA cases); Ruth Colker, *Winning and losing under the Americans with Disabilities Act*, 62 OHIO ST. L.J. 239, 242, 2001, showing that most ADA cases brought on appeal result in defendant-friendly outcomes; see also Julie L. Hotchkiss, 'A closer look at

with disabilities steadily declined throughout the 1990s.[11] The Kessler Foundation and NOD commissioned Harris Interactive to conduct the 2010 Survey of Americans with Disabilities.[12] The new data were compared with those from surveys conducted over the past twenty-four years, measuring the gaps in experiences and attitudes between people with and without disabilities. The survey solicited feedback in ten important areas: employment, income, education, healthcare, access to transportation, socialising, dining out in restaurants, attendance at religious services, political participation and life satisfaction. The survey also featured three new indicators: technology use, access to mental health services and general financial situation.

Overall, findings demonstrated modest improvement in a few areas, although most indicators showed little or no change in the twenty years since the ADA was enacted.[13] Employment remains responsible for the largest gap between people with and without disabilities. Among working-age people with disabilities, only 21 percent reported working either full- or part-time, compared with 59 percent of people without disabilities – a gap of 38 percentage points. This gap has decreased from 43 percent since it was first examined in 1998, but it remains large and its decline has been slow. Education and political participation are the two areas where the gaps have narrowed.

It is quite difficult to measure the impact of a major civil rights statute.[14] Outcome depends upon a complex process of implementation by courts, enforcement agencies and employers.[15] Furthermore, it is impossible to detach the status of civil rights from other social and

the employment impact of the Americans with Disabilities Act', *Journal of Human Resources* 39 (2004), 887–911.

[11] See, for example, Thomas DeLeire, 'The wage and employment effects of the Americans with Disabilities Act', *Journal of Human Resources* 35 (2000), 693–715; Daron Acemoglu and Joshua Angrist, 'Consequences of employment protection? The case of the Americans with Disabilities Act', *Journal of Political Economy* 109 (2001), 915–57.

[12] Can be accessed at www.2010DisabilitySurveys.org.

[13] See complete survey data at www.2010DisabilitySurveys.org.

[14] John J. Donohue III and James Heckman, 'Continuous versus episodic change: The impact of civil rights policy on the economic status of blacks', *Journal of Economic Literature* 29 (1991), 1603–43.

[15] See, for example, A. W. Blumrosen, *Modern law: The law transmission system and equal employment opportunity* (Madison, WI: University of Wisconsin Press, 1993).

economic factors such as labour market conditions or/and government regulation in interrelated areas.[16] Finally, the definition of disability in the ADA's employment provisions is narrow and can be misleading in interpreting employment outcomes.[17]

What is the contribution of the ADA for people with disabilities? Do workers with disabilities exercise their rights in the workplace? Filing an ADA complaint is one of the mechanisms people with disabilities can use to defend their rights. The number of workers who filed discrimination claims under the ADA in the decade after the statute was passed exceeds 200,000; however, only a small number proceeded with their claims.[18] Research on the ADA suggests that people with disabilities are familiar with the law but cannot exercise their rights for a variety of reasons, such as difficulties accessing a lawyer or coping with psychological and social barriers. It seems that there is a significant gap between their intentions and the fact that they will need to cope with issues themselves without adequate assistance and acceptance.[19]

Are employers familiar with the ADA's reasonable accommodations provisions for workers with disabilities? Existing data show that employers are aware of accommodations for people with disabilities, and the majority of federal and private respondents report that they have received training in this area.[20] Here again it is disappointing that awareness has not translated into significant gains in the hiring practices for people with disabilities.

---

[16] James J. Heckman, 'The central role of the South in accounting for the economic progress of black Americans', *The American Economic Review* 80 (1990), 242–6.

[17] See discussion on the disability definition of the ADA in two publications: Peter Blanck, Susan Schwochau and Chen Song, 'Is it time to declare the ADA a failed law?' In *The decline in employment of people with disabilities: A policy puzzle*. Edited by David Stapleton and Richard Burkhauser (Kalamazoo, MI: W. E. Upjohn Institute for Employment Research, 2003), pp. 301–37; Douglas Kruse and Lisa Schur, 'Employment of people with disabilities following the ADA', *Industrial Relations* 42 (2003), 31–64.

[18] For an extensive review see Kathryn Moss, 'Unfunded mandate: An empirical study of the implementation of the Americans with Disabilities Act by the Equal Employment Opportunity Commission', *Kansas Law Review* 50 (2005), 1–110.

[19] Ibid.

[20] See Susanne M. Bruyere, William A. Erickson and Sara A. VanLooy, 'Impact of business size on employer ADA response', *Rehabilitation Counseling Bulletin* 49 (2006), 194–206.

Unfortunately, Title I of the ADA has had only modest success in the courts and lacks poor administrative enforcement.[21] ADA case law is being made on a case-by-case basis and not as class-protected action. It is not enough for the plaintiff to show that he or she has a medical condition that, as a general matter, is plainly a disability. Rather, the person has to prove to the court exactly how this condition constitutes a substantial limitation of a major activity yet does not prevent him or her from being employable.

In three significant cases involving nearsightedness, hypertension and monocular vision, the U.S. Supreme Court held that mitigating or corrective measures should be considered in determining whether an individual has a disability under the ADA.[22] The Supreme Court used a restricted view of disability, meaning that an employer may discriminate against someone because he or she has, for example, diabetes, but as long as the victim is successfully controlling the condition with medication he or she has no recourse under the ADA.

Another demonstration of the Supreme Court's restricted interpretation of disability is evident in the case of *Toyota v. Williams*.[23] The court did not deny that the plaintiff suffered from carpal tunnel syndrome for many years and had changed job assignments several times because of it. However, the court ruled that it 'substantially' excluded 'impairments

---

[21] See Louis S. Rulli and Jason A. Leckerman, 'Unfinished business: The fading promise of ADA enforcement in the federal courts under Title I and its impact on the poor', *Journal of Gender, Race and Justice* 8 (2005), 595, 652.

[22] See three U.S. Supreme Court decisions: in *Sutton v. United Airlines, Inc.*, 527 U.S. 471, 119 S. Ct. 2139 (June 22, 1999), the Supreme Court held that the determination of whether a person has an ADA 'disability' must take into consideration whether the person is substantially limited in a major life activity when using a mitigating measure such as medication, a prosthesis or a hearing aid. A person who experiences no substantial limitation in any major life activity when using a mitigating measure does not meet the ADA's definition of 'disability'; in *Murphy v. United Parcel Service, Inc.*, 527 U.S. 516, 119 S. Ct. 2133 (1999), the Supreme Court followed Sutton to find that a person whose high blood pressure was controlled through medication did not have an impairment that substantially limited a major life activity; in *Albertsons, Inc. v. Kirkingburg*, 527 U.S. 555, 119 S. Ct. 2162 (1999), the Supreme Court extended the analysis in Sutton and Murphy to include individuals who specifically develop compensating behaviors to mitigate the effects of an impairment. In this case, the Supreme Court found that individuals with monocular vision could develop compensating behaviors that would prevent the impairment from substantially limiting the major life activity of seeing.

[23] *Toyota Motor Manufacturing, Kentucky, Inc. v. Williams*, 'Case citation' 534 U.S. 184 (2002).

that interfere in only a minor way' with activity and narrowed 'major life activity' to mean one that is of '*central importance* to daily life'.[24] Despite her undisputed impairment and the demonstrable limitations that it created, the plaintiff failed to qualify as disabled because 'she could still brush her teeth, wash her face, bathe, tend her flower garden, fix breakfast, do laundry, and pick up around the house'.[25]

Interestingly, the Supreme Court's interpretation implies that for many people with disabilities, taking medication or using devices means that they are not substantially limited in the activities of daily life. The same restrictive definition was given by the U.S. Supreme Court in the *Sutton, Murphy* and *Williams* cases in which the Court cast serious doubt on this, suggesting that if the only activity impaired was working, then the plaintiff would need to show that he or she was 'unable to work in a broad class of jobs'.[26]

Series of annual studies conducted by the editors of the *Mental and Physical Disability Law Reporter* have analysed Title I final case decisions in federal courts.[27] They have demonstrated how rarely plaintiffs secure a favourable court judgment or jury verdict in published ADA case decisions. In terms of reversals on appeal, the plaintiff success rate in these cases ranged from just under 8 percent between 1992 and 1997 to as low as 3 percent from 2002 to 2004.

Another study of published appellate decisions found that courts ruled in favour of defendants in most of the cases (94 percent).[28] Courts of

---

[24] Ibid., 194.

[25] Ibid., 202.

[26] Ibid., *Sutton v. United Airlines, Inc.*, 1999; *Murphy v. United Parcel Service*, 1999; *Toyota Motor Manufacturing, Kentucky, Inc. v. Williams*, 2002.

[27] See series of studies by Amy L. Allbright, 'Employment decisions under the ADA Title I – survey update', *Mental & Physical Disability Law Reporter* 25 (2001), 508–10; 'Employment decisions under the ADA Title I – survey update', *Mental & Physical Disability Law Reporter* 26 (2002), 394–8; 'Employment decisions under the ADA Title I – survey update', *Mental & Physical Disability Law Reporter* 27 (2003), 387–9; 'Survey update: 2003 employer-employee wins under ADA Title I', *Mental & Physical Disability Law Reporter* 28 (2004), 319; '2004 employment decisions under the ADA Title I – survey update', *Mental & Physical Disability Law Reporter* 29 (2005), 513–16 and two studies by J. W. Parry, 'Trend: Employment decisions under the ADA Title I – survey update, *Mental & Physical Disability Law Reporter* 23 (1999), 294–8; 'Employment decisions under the ADA Title I – survey update', *Mental & Physical Disability Law Reporter* 24 (2000), 348–50.

[28] Colker, *The Americans with Disabilities Act: A windfall for defendants*.

appeals reversed pro-defendant outcomes in trial courts only 21 percent of the time in Title I cases, whereas the rates were 26 percent to 48 percent in other types of cases. There was a similar gap in appellate reversals of trial court decisions in favour of plaintiffs in ADA cases.

However, it seems that reported case decisions are not a reliable measure of overall outcomes because most lawsuits are settled without a reported decision. An interesting study of federal court files on a nationally representative sample of 4,114 lawsuits filed between 1993 and 2001, which linked the cases with administrative data obtained from the U.S. Equal Employment Opportunity Commission (EEOC), found that almost two-thirds of cases were classified as settlements.[29] The majority of people eligible to file a Title I lawsuit in federal court did not invoke this right, and 87 percent of employment claims filed with state and federal agencies were abandoned without a resolution.

On 25 September 2008, President George W. Bush signed the Americans with Disabilities Amendments Act of 2008. The act makes important changes to the restricted definition of disability by rejecting the findings in several Supreme Court decisions.[30] The effect of these changes is to make it easier for an individual seeking protection under the ADA to establish that he or she has a disability within the meaning of the ADA.

It is too early to determine the impact of the ADA Amendments Act of 2008 on hiring practices. The revised definition of disability aims to more broadly encompass impairments that substantially limit a major life activity. Mitigating measures, including assistive devices, auxiliary aids, accommodations, medical therapies and supplies have no bearing in determining whether a disability qualifies under the law. The clarification of impairments that are episodic or in remission that substantially limit a major life activity when active, such as epilepsy or post-traumatic stress disorder, all raise the expectation that more people with disabilities will qualify under the ADA.

---

[29] See Kevin Barry, 'Toward universalism: What the ADA Amendments Act of 2008 can and can't do for disability rights', *Berkeley Journal of Employment and Labor Law*, 31 (2010), 203–83.

[30] Bruyere et al., 'Impact of business size on employer ADA response'.

THE UK DISABILITY DISCRIMINATION ACT OF 1995/2005 AND THE EQUALITY ACT OF 2010

The development of laws against discrimination in the UK since the 1960s has been piecemeal, resulting in numerous acts of parliament and sets of regulations. The first piece of legislation dealing directly with disability discrimination, the DDA of 1995, was enacted five years after the ADA and was subject to significant amendments over the following twelve or so years, and case law has had a great impact on how the law works. This legislation was extended in 2005 and replaced recently by new legislation, the Equality Act of 2010.[31]

THE UK DISABILITY DISCRIMINATION ACT OF 1995

The Disability Discrimination Act of 1995 makes it unlawful to discriminate against those with a disability when providing services and for most employers when providing employment.[32] The legislation imposes an obligation on service providers not to discriminate against people with disabilities in the provision of goods or services, or in employment.

The Act has several sections:

Part I: Identifies who is covered by the Act. Their impairment has to have a substantial and long-term effect on their daily activities. This includes: people with long-term health conditions such as diabetes; people with progressive conditions such as MS, HIV or cancer;[33] people with learning disabilities; people with mental health conditions; people with mobility difficulties, including wheelchair users; blind and partially sighted people; deaf and hearing impaired people; and elderly people who think of their impairment as part of the ageing process.

Part II: Covers the employment of people with a disability and applies to all employers. This section imposes an obligation to carry out physical adjustments to a place of work or adjustments to work duties for an

---

[31] See for extensive review, Anna Lawson, *Disability and equality law in Britain: The role of reasonable adjustment* (Oxford: Hart Publishing, 2008).

[32] Can be accessed at http://www.legislation.gov.uk/ukpga/1995/50/contents.

[33] DDA 2005 covers these conditions from point of diagnosis.

employee with a disability. Work only needs to be reactive.[34] Funding is available to meet most of the costs over £300, administered via the local Jobcentre Plus.

Part III: Covers the duties of service providers. The duties of service providers are: not to treat disabled people less favourably than others for a reason relating to their disability; not to provide services on worse terms than for other people (e.g., charge more for services); to make 'reasonable adjustments' to policies, practices and procedures; to provide auxiliary equipment where appropriate; and to make reasonable adjustments to premises to facilitate physical access. Service providers should anticipate that goods and services will be required by people with a disability and should make anticipatory adjustments, not waiting until a disabled person advises that the service can't be used by them. Information produced by a service provider, Web sites and means of communication all need to be designed with all users in mind. The final duties imposed by the Act came into force on 1 October 2004, and require 'reasonable' adjustments to be made to services to give access to people with physical, sensory or learning impairments. There are no grants available to cover the cost of work, but costs may be claimed as a revenue or capital expense by a business. Individual disabled people who have been discriminated against can bring a civil action through the courts and may receive support from the Disability Rights Commission.

Part IV: Covers the duties of education providers and was reinforced by the Special Educational Needs and Disability Act (SENDA 2001).[35] Duties imposed under SENDA are similar to those under Part III of the Act and came fully into force in October 2005.

Part V: Covers means of transport such as coaches, buses and trains. There are extensive technical requirements for the design of new vehicles with time frames extended to 2016 to 2020 for all vehicles to comply with these requirements. Train and bus stations and other infrastructures are covered by Part III of the Act.

What is the impact of the DDA in eliminating discrimination toward people with disabilities? Does the law contribute to their inclusion in the

---

[34] That is, carried out when employees require it due to their disability.

[35] Special Educational Needs and Disability Act (SENDA 2001) can be accessed at http://www.legislation.gov.uk/ukpga/2001/10/contents.

workplace? The general expectation is that the law will reduce barriers to employment and increase employment rates.[36] An important review of the DDA in comparison to the ADA reveals that the British law has received little attention.[37] Among the possible reasons for lack of impact on the employment rate of people with disabilities are low take-up of financial support, lack of awareness among disabled people and employers and limited knowledge about the costs of required adjustments.

Another comprehensive report evaluated the achievements of the DDA ten years later and found that the legislation enabled thousands of people with disabilities to gain some financial redress at the employment tribunals. However, the general conclusion is that the act has failed to adequately tackle and reduce employment discrimination.[38]

Among the problems reported by the Public Interest Research Unit were cases of prejudice, institutional discrimination and significantly lower wages among individuals with disabilities. Specifically, the research identified a number of factors as helping to explain the limits to the success of the DDA's employment provisions. With respect to employees with disabilities, they have demonstrated a low level of awareness and poor understanding of the act. Many expressed difficulties in initiating the application, scepticism about the expected results and fear of victimisation.

The report also revealed that claims were unlikely to succeed. For example, in 2004 to 2005, 236 DDA employment claims succeeded at tribunal, while 4,437 were dropped, settled through ACAS or failed at tribunal. The main reason was that disability has been narrowly defined by the law and has prevented individuals with unrecognised disabilities from receiving support for their discrimination case. Similarly to the ADA,

---

[36] For extensive review, see Daniel Pope and Clare Bambra, 'Has the Disability Discrimination Act closed the employment gap?' *Disability and Rehabilitation* 27 (2005), 1261–6; Caroline Gooding, 'Disability Discrimination Act: From statute to practice', *Critical Social Policy* 20 (2000), 533–49.

[37] David Bell and Axel Heitmueller, 'The Disability Discrimination Act in the UK: Helping or hindering employment amongst the disabled?' Bonn: The Institute for the Study of Labor (IZA), Discussion Paper No 1476, 2005. Accessed 12 October 2010, ftp://repec.iza.org/RePEc/Discussionpaper/dp1476.pdf.

[38] The report was published in 2005 by the Public Interest Research Unit and is entitled *The end of the beginning – a critical analysis of the first decade of the Disability Discrimination Act employment provisions.* Accessed 22 November 2011, www.leeds.ac.uk/disability-studies/archiveuk/harwood/eobbl.pdf.

the definition continues to exclude a large percentage of individuals with severe, life-limiting impairments and to discriminate against those with particular illnesses and disabilities. In addition, substantial numbers of claimants appear to have lost their cases as a result of incorrect, and sometimes inept, interpretations of the legislation.

The ten-year report found that employers were unlikely to be deterred. They wrongly assumed that the employment provisions of the DDA did not apply to them. They tended to overestimate the potential costs of compliance with the Act and underestimated the potential benefits for the workplace. The report criticised the looseness and ambiguity of the legislation and the need to clarify and tighten the duties of public authorities. For example, it was unclear how a public authority would be found not to have 'due regard' for 'equality of opportunity' when there was no definition of what this term should be taken to mean. The legislation excluded many organisations that had a considerable impact on the lives of people with disabilities from their obligations. Lastly, the enforcement was quite poor and lacked adequate resources.

The Disability Discrimination Act 2005 is actually the extension of the DDA of 1995 covering earlier unresolved issues of public transport and the introduction of a responsibility on public authorities to promote equality for people with disabilities. In terms of transport, operators have been asked to meet Part III obligations for transport services in the use of a bus or train as air and sea transport is currently regulated by a voluntary agreement of the carriers.

The public authorities component called upon public bodies to take into account the rights of people with disabilities as an integral part of their policies, practices and procedures. They were called upon to eliminate unlawful discrimination and disability-related harassment, promote equality of opportunity and positive attitudes to disabled people and encourage people with disabilities to take part in public life.

Many public bodies, including government departments and local councils, were required to produce a Disability Equality Scheme explaining how they intended to fulfil the duty to promote equality. Public bodies were asked to think through the implications of the duty and gather appropriate evidence to demonstrate the effectiveness of their schemes. Public bodies had to demonstrate that people with disabilities were part of their planning processes and procedures.

The Equality Act of 2010 (EA)[39] aims to streamline and strengthen antidiscrimination legislation and provides the legal framework that protects all people from discrimination. It replaces a range of antidiscrimination legislation, including the DDA (1995), and is intended to be easier to operate and understand than previous equality legislation. The Act provides a legal framework of equality law for all people with 'protected characteristics', including disability, age, race and gender.

Specifically, there are few core differences in comparison to the DDA (1995). First, the definition of disability in the EA is slightly different, defining a person with disability as someone who has a mental or physical impairment that has a substantial and long-term adverse effect on the person's ability to carry out normal day-to-day activities. *Disability*, according to the DDA, required also that the person with a disability would show that an adversely affected normal day-to-day activity involved one of a list of capacities such as mobility, speech or hearing. Second, the DDA limited its protection from direct discrimination only in employment and related areas, whereas the EA also protects people with disabilities against direct discrimination in areas beyond the employment field (such as the supply of goods, facilities and services). Third, the EA introduces improved protection from discrimination that occurs because of something connected with a person's disability. This form of discrimination can be justified if it can be shown to be a proportionate means of achieving a legitimate aim. Fourth, the EA introduces the principle of indirect discrimination for disability. Fifth, the EA applies one trigger point at which there is a duty to make reasonable adjustments for people with disability. This trigger is in cases where the person with a disability would be at a substantial disadvantage compared to a person without a disability if the adjustment were not made. Sixth, the EA extends protection from harassment that is related to disability. Seventh, the EA contains a new provision that limits the type of enquiries that a recruiting employer can make about disability and health when recruiting new staff. This provision tries to eliminate unfairly screening out of the disabled person at an early stage of the recruitment process.

---

[39] Equality Act (EA) 2010 can be accessed at http://www.legislation.gov.uk/ukpga/2010/15/contents.

However, there are concerns raised by the business community that this legislation means excessive regulation during a very bad economic time and that small businesses would experience additional difficulties. According to the British Chambers of Commerce (BCC), the Equality Act of 2010 will have a one-off net cost of £189.2 million to businesses, and the adult national minimum wage (NMW) will rise by 13p to £5.93 per hour, with both the development rate and the youth rate also increasing. From now on, apprentices will also be entitled to an NMW of £2.50 per hour.[40]

ISRAEL'S EQUAL RIGHTS FOR PERSONS WITH DISABILITIES LAW OF 1998: AN IN-DEPTH VIEW

The Israeli equal rights legislation for persons with disabilities is a very good example of international disability legislation associated with the ADA and the DDA. Israel is a fairly small country and enacted the law eight years after the ADA and three years after the DDA (1995) in the UK. As in most Western European countries, the Israeli legislation prior to the enactment of the Equal Rights for Persons with Disability Law was related to social benefits and marginally to disability rights issues such as accessibility.[41] For example, the primary piece of legislation concerning accessibility was a piecemeal amendment made in 1981 to the Planning and Building Law together with the accompanying regulations. Because the scheme applies only to buildings, places open to the public that are not buildings (such as public parks, cemeteries, etc.) are exempt, as well as services designated for public use such as transport, cultural and recreational facilities or banking services. A similar limit to accessibility in old laws is found in the Special Provisions for Deaf Persons Law enacted in 1992.[42]

There is no doubt that the passage of the ADA in 1990 had a significant effect on the enactment of Israeli disability rights legislation. In

---

[40] See http://www.businesswest.co.uk/about_us/media_coverage/pr_-_business_wants_less_regul. aspx.

[41] Equal Rights for Persons with Disabilities Law, 5758–1998 (1999), can be accessed at http://www.justice.gov.il/structure/foreign/files_eng.htm.

[42] The Special Provisions for Deaf Persons Law, enacted in 1992; subtitling is limited to a mere 25 percent of non-live television broadcasts.

1998, the Israeli Knesset (parliament) passed the first three sections of the new Equal Rights for Persons with Disabilities Law (Transportation, Employment and Disability Ombudsman), leaving seven additional sections for future legislation (Accessibility; Housing in the Community and Personal Assistance; Education; Culture, Leisure and Sport; Special Needs; the Court System; General).

The two opening chapters of the Equal Rights Law, entitled Fundamental Principles and General Principles, laid the constitutional grounds for ensuing operative provisions on employment, accessibility and the Equal Rights Commission. Couched in the language of a Basic Law, the initial sections of the law enshrine the basic right of a person with disabilities to equality, human dignity and active participation in society in all walks of life. Patronising interference with personal autonomy has been replaced by the right of a person with disabilities to make decisions regarding his or her own life. Another fundamental principle is the legitimacy of affirmative action programmes where persons with disabilities are concerned. The General Principles chapter also establishes the universal right of a person with disabilities to exercise his or her rights within the existing institutions of society as opposed to segregated frameworks.

In defining its constituent population, the Equal Rights Law embraces the holistic approach embodied in the paradigm shift by defining a 'person with a disability' as 'a person with a physical, emotional or mental disability, including a cognitive disability, permanent or temporary, as a result of which that person's functioning is substantially limited in one or more of the major spheres of life'.[43] This definition emphasises the person first and disability second, whereas the previous legislation referred primarily to the person's impairment and illness.

At the heart of the chapters on the law on employment, public transport services and other public places and services is the adoption of a broad definition of discrimination. Thus, the prohibition on discrimination in all of these areas includes, but is not limited to, failure to make reasonable accommodations which will enable persons with disabilities to integrate into the world of work and to access public places and services as others do.

Expanding on the proactive approach embodied in the obligation to make reasonable accommodations, a reasonable accommodation does not

---

[43] Ibid.; Equal Rights for Persons with Disabilities Law, 5758–1998.

change the essential functions of the job. Whether a particular accommodation request is reasonable depends upon the situation and the type of job. The accommodation cannot be extremely costly or disruptive for the employer.

The employment chapter requires the civil service and other employers with more than twenty-five employees to promote 'appropriate representation' of persons with disabilities in the work force. In addition to the prohibition on discrimination, the duty to make reasonable accommodations and the obligation to promote appropriate representation, the Equal Rights for Persons with Disabilities Law requires the state to provide practical assistance to equal-opportunity employers: Regulations under the law provide for substantial, albeit partial, financing by the state of employment accommodations.

Following the 2005 amendment to the Law, the bulk of its numerous sections is devoted to the new accessibility regime: As part of the prohibition on disability-based discrimination in the operation of public places and the provision of public services, the Law now requires that these be made accessible in such a way that persons with physical, sensory, psychiatric, mental, cognitive and developmental disabilities will be able to benefit to the full from public services and will be able to enter a public place, move around and fully enjoy its facilities. The accessibility requirement applies to public places and services operated by the state and other public authorities, as well as to those operated by the private sector. Existing buildings, as well as entirely new construction, must be made accessible. The vast array of accommodations is to be set out in a series of detailed regulations.

Determined that the Equal Rights Law would not be a 'dead letter', the Knesset adopted the Katz Commission's unequivocal recommendation to establish a central state-funded body, the Commission for Equal Rights of Persons with Disabilities, whose express statutory mission is to promote the fundamental principles of the law and to enforce its operative provisions. The commission's enforcement role has been enhanced by virtue of the 2005 amendment: In addition to filing a civil claim for violation of the provisions of the employment chapter in relation to violation of accessibility provisions, the commission may either file a civil claim or, subject to providing notice as required by the Law, issue an accessibility order setting out the various steps required in order to make a particular place or service accessible, together with a time frame for so doing. The Law provides for the appointment of a sole commissioner to head the commission, along with an advisory committee to the commission, a majority of whose members are persons with disabilities.

The enactment of the Equal Rights Law in 1998 was followed by a new generation of rights-based statutes and amendments in various fields.[44] The enactment of the accessibility amendment to the Equal Rights Law in March 2005 was followed by the passage of the Broadcasting Television Law (Subtitles and Signing).[45]

Throughout the legislative process determined efforts were made primarily by persons with disabilities and their organisations to ensure that the Equal Rights Law would be put into practice. One of the recent amendments that has been passed is related to accessibility of public buildings.[46] Due to the substantial costs of making existing public buildings and infrastructure accessible, long periods of gradual implementation have been prescribed. The public sector has been given the exceptionally long period of twelve years (eleven years in the case of health services and emergency services), in view of the wide range of places and services for which the public sector is responsible and the extremely narrow scope of exemptions enjoyed by anybody financed by the public purse. The

[44] The Law for the Rehabilitation of Persons with Psychiatric Disabilities in the Community (2000) establishes the right of a person with a psychiatric disability to a comprehensive rehabilitation program. The Day Rehabilitation Centers Law (2000) provides for the right of a young, severely disabled child aged one to three years to treatment and education at a special day rehabilitation centre. An amendment to the Property Law passed in 2001 provides the statutory framework for making accommodations to the common parts of apartment buildings, in some cases without even the consent of other residents. An extensive amendment to the Special Education Law passed in 2002 makes a series of provisions for the right of children with disabilities to integrate into the regular school system.

[45] The Broadcasting Television Law (Subtitles and Signing), 5765–2005 (hereinafter: 'the Subtitles and Signing Law'). The new law, which replaces the 1992 Deaf Persons Relief Law, applies broader responsibilities and restrictions on broadcasters in order to enhance, to the fullest extent possible, disabled peoples' accessibility to television broadcasts.

[46] In 2005, the Law was amended again to add section E1 – Public Places and Public Services. This section incorporated many new and important elements: prohibition of discrimination in public services, public places and products; accessibility of public places and public services; restrictions on the statutory duty of accessibility; and accessibility to education and higher education institutions and education services. Furthermore, this section introduced regulations regarding insurance contracts, road accessibility, accessibility to emergency services, accessibility to public transportation, state participation in financing adjustments, accessibility coordinators, authorised personnel, authorities of the commissioner, penalties, legal prosecution and other issues. The Law was amended again in 2007.

private sector on the other hand, to which the economic exemption of an 'undue burden' is available, has been given a much shorter and gradual implementation period of six years.

Implementation is considerably more advanced where accessibility of public transport services is concerned. Because this had a 'head start' by being included in the original Equal Rights Law of 1998, there are regulations in place, albeit they were published only in 2003. The Transport Accessibility Regulations also provide for gradual implementation over periods ranging from two to ten years in relation to trains, aircrafts and boats. Buses produced from 2002 have to be made accessible.

Whilst the new accessibility regime is, for the most part, still in the process of being established, the potential created by the Equal Rights Law for its enforcement, once in place, is immense. Persons with disabilities, the Equal Rights Commissions, NGOs and others will be able to activate a wide variety of enforcement mechanisms that are both preventative and reactive in nature. Building permits and business licenses relating to public places and services will be conditional upon the approval of a licensed accessibility expert, stating that all the relevant accessibility requirements have been met. In additional to the Commission's special powers to issue accessibility orders, persons with disabilities or a disability-rights NGO may file an individual civil claim or a class action suit with a view to making a public place or service accessible in accordance with the regulations. Should the court uphold the claim, it may, in addition to the usual remedies (injunction and/or damages), award punitive damages without proof of actual damage.

As opposed to the new accessibility regime, the employment provisions of the Equal Rights Law have been on the statute books since 1998, and entered into force in 1999. In the thirteen years that have passed since then, it would seem reasonable to expect to see an improvement in the employment situation of persons with disabilities as a result of the Law. However, similar to findings related to the ADA, the evidence shows that the high unemployment figures for persons with disabilities that were obtained prior to the passage of the Law remain unchanged.[47] For example, among recipients of the general disability benefit from the

---

[47] Arie Rimmerman and Shirley Avrami, 'Israel's Equal Rights for Persons with Disabilities Law: Legal base, process and impact', *International Journal of Disability, Community & Rehabilitation* 8 (2010). Accessed 11 October 2011, http://www.ijdcr.ca.

Israeli National Insurance Institute (Israel's version of Social Security) aged eighteen to sixty-five, only 15 percent are in an employment framework, only 10 percent are employed in supported employment positions in the open market, and the rest are in sheltered employment.[48]

Experts estimate, however, that at least 40 percent of those in sheltered employment frameworks are capable of integrating into supported employment, which would give them the opportunity to work in the open market.[49] Disappointment with the apparent failure of Israeli law in the employment field would seem to be mirrored by the American experience. It is now generally accepted that the ADA has not resulted in the substantial employment gains for individuals with disabilities that its proponents had predicted.[50]

There are few cases that reflect the success of the employment chapter of the law. The duty to make reasonable accommodations was the subject of the *Steinberg* case decided in 2003.[51] The Labour Court decision was that it is the employer's duty to find alternative suitable employment for an employee who has become disabled during the course of his employment. In contrast to the American experience, the definition of a 'person with a disability' has arisen in only one decided case, that of De Castro Dekel, in which it was held that an employee with cancer was a person with a disability.[52] Taking these cases, together with the substantially delayed promulgation of the regulations concerning state financing of accommodations in 2006, and failure to set regulations concerning appropriate representation, it is clear that the full potential for implementation of the employment provisions of the Equal Rights Law has yet to be realised.

Implementation of the third and final operative part of the Equal Rights Law, concerning the establishment of the Equal Rights Commission, has also proven to be a gradual, long-term process. The Commission was established in August 2000 and has been active since then in a number of areas, including the promotion of cooperation between the various

---

[48] State Comptroller, *Annual Report 52b—Integrating people with disabilities in society and in employment* (Jerusalem: Government Press Office, 29 April 2002) (Hebrew), pp. 163–91.

[49] Avital Sandler Loeff, Nurit Strosberg and Denise Naon, *People with disabilities in Israel: Facts and figures* (Jerusalem: JDC-Brookdale Institute, 2003).

[50] Barbara A. Lee, 'A decade of the Americans with Disabilities Act: Judicial outcomes and unresolved problems', *Industrial Relations* 42 (2003), 11–30.

[51] 3706/03; 5712/03 *Steinberg v. Israel Electric Company*, Tel Aviv District Labor Court (3.12.03) (Hebrew).

[52] 1732/04 *De Castro Dekel v. M.B.A. Hazorea* (10.7.05) (Hebrew).

bodies (public, private and voluntary) active in the field; expansion of accessibility to public places and services, including public transport; adaptation of emergency services to the needs of people with disabilities; commissioning research and surveys; taking an active role in the formulation of new legislation; and public relations campaigns raising awareness in the field of accessibility and of the rights of people with disabilities in general. The Commission has faced political and administrative challenges. There have been political pressures from disability groups to set the Commission's agenda and to strengthen the role of the advisory committee. The Commission's moderate budget is another obstacle in maintaining and expanding its central role.

An account of the principal perceptible effects of the Equal Rights Law would not be complete without mentioning its impact on areas that are not the subject of any specific statutory provision. The Law has profoundly changed the nature of public discourse concerning persons with disabilities. Public authorities now employ the language of human rights in this context, a fact evidenced by the State Comptroller's Report of 2002.[53] Dealing with the integration of persons with disabilities in the workplace and in society at large, the comprehensive findings and conclusions of the comptroller paint a bleak picture.

However the comptroller's standpoint throughout is that of advocate for the fundamental rights enshrined in the Equal Rights Law. It was these fundamental rights that guided the Supreme Court on the eve of the 1999 general elections, when it ordered the state to produce a quick and effective solution to the inaccessibility of most polling stations in Israel. The solution, which allows for persons with disabilities to vote in any accessible polling station wherever that may be, was later put on a statutory footing in an amendment to the Knesset Elections Law.

CONCLUSION: THE IMPACT OF DOMESTIC DISABILITY RIGHTS LAWS ON SOCIAL INCLUSION

Until the 1960s, people with disabilities were perceived as incapable of coping with society at large. In most Western countries, including the

---

[53] State Comptroller, *Annual Report 52b*—29 April 2002, pp. 163–91.

United States, the UK and Israel, disability was addressed as an aspect of social security and welfare legislation, health law or guardianship.[54] People with disabilities were viewed not as citizens with legal rights but as objects of welfare, health and charity programmes. Unfortunately, this social policy approach contributed indirectly to their exclusion and segregation from mainstream society into special schools, sheltered workshops and housing.

The ADA was a watershed event for disability rights on the international stage. The ADA recognised that discrimination against people with disabilities in the form of purposeful unequal treatment and historical patterns of segregation and isolation was the major problem confronting people with disabilities, not their individual impairments. As such, the ADA bars discrimination against people with disabilities in employment, public services, public accommodations and telecommunications.

However, although the ADA forbids employment discrimination, the fact is that post-ADA Americans with disabilities continue to experience disproportionately high rates of unemployment. Similar evidence has been recorded in the UK as the DDA has not much changed the employment status of people with disabilities. Similarly, the Israeli legislation has not been translated into practical gains in employment and social and civic participation. There is recognition that using equality and social justice language is remarkable, but people with disabilities require both resources and the opportunity to utilise those resources to achieve their potential. The Israeli disability rights legislation and probably the ADA as well, will be judged in years to come by their abilities to contribute to the full inclusion of people with disabilities into society.

---

[54] For further reading, see Jerome E. Bickenbach, 'Disability human rights, law and policy'. In *Handbook of Disability Studies*. Edited by Gary Albrecht, Katherine Seelman and Michael Bury (Thousand Oaks, CA: Sage Publications, 2001), pp. 565–84; Diane Driedger, *The last civil rights movement. Disabled people's international* (London: Hurst and Company, 1989); Victor Florian and Nira Dangor, 'Main issues in the rehabilitation in Israel', *Society & Welfare* 19 (1999), pp. 193–212 (Hebrew); Patrick Fougeyrollas and Line Beauregard, 'The interactive person-environment in disability in creation'. In *Handbook of disability studies*. Edited by Gary Albrecht, Katherine Seelman and Michael Bury, pp. 171–94; Richard K. Scotch, *From good will to civil rights: Transforming federal disability policy* (Philadelphia: Temple University Press, 1984).

7 THE CONVENTION ON THE RIGHTS OF PERSONS WITH DISABILITIES: A COMPREHENSIVE INSTRUMENT TO PROMOTE SOCIAL INCLUSION

The work of the UN constitutes the most important actions taken by an international organisation to promote social inclusion of people with disabilities. The first document that addressed their rights was the 1971 Declaration on the Rights of Mentally Retarded Persons.[1] This declaration was based on the International Bill of Rights formulated earlier by the UN.[2]

Following the 1971 Declaration, there have been other important documents that built up the foundations for future promotion of rights, but none of them have been legally binding. In 1981, the UN General Assembly declared the first International Year of Disabled Persons,[3] which was followed by the World Programme of Action Concerning Disabled Persons in 1982 and the Decade of Disabled Persons 1983–1992. Throughout the 1990s, all UN conferences dealt with disability rights and addressed the need for protective instruments. A high level of awareness

---

[1] Declaration on the Rights of Mentally Retarded Persons, G.A. res. 2856 (XXVI), 26 U.N. GAOR Supp. (No. 29) at 93, U.N. Doc. A/8429 (1971).

[2] Universal Declaration of Human Rights (Article 1), adopted by General Assembly resolution 217 A (III) of 10 December 1948.

[3] In 1976, the UN General Assembly proclaimed 1981 as the International Year of Disabled Persons (IYDP). It called for a plan of action at the national, regional and international levels, with an emphasis on equalisation of opportunities, rehabilitation and prevention of disabilities. The theme of IYDP was 'full participation and equality', defined as the right of persons with disabilities to take part fully in the life and development of their societies, enjoy living conditions equal to those of other citizens and have an equal share in improved conditions resulting from socioeconomic development. Other objectives of the year included: increasing public awareness; understanding and acceptance of persons who are disabled; and encouraging persons with disabilities to form organisations through which they can express their views and promote action to improve their situation.

was also demonstrated by the EU, which declared the year 2003 the European Year of People with Disabilities.[4]

DEVELOPMENT OF THE UN CONVENTION ON THE RIGHTS OF PERSONS WITH DISABILITIES

The Convention on the Rights of Persons with Disabilities (CRPD) is an international human rights instrument that was drafted and negotiated between 2002 and 2006, and is intended to protect the rights and dignity of persons with disabilities.[5] The text was adopted by the UN General Assembly on 13 December 2006 and signed on 31 March 2007. Following ratification it came into force on 3 May 2008 and was subsequently ratified by almost all countries.

GUIDING PRINCIPLES OF THE CRPD

The UN CRPD is the most comprehensive global effort to protect the rights of people with disabilities and ensure within their states their social inclusion and full participation. Article 1 states that its purpose is

> to promote, protect and ensure the full and equal enjoyment of all human rights and fundamental freedoms by all persons with disabilities, and to promote respect for their inherent dignity. Persons with disabilities include those who have long-term physical, mental, intellectual or sensory impairments, which in interaction with various barriers may hinder their full and effective participation in society on an equal basis with others.[6]

---

[4] Also called the European Year of Disabled People.

[5] See the National Council on Disability (NCD), 'Finding the gaps: A comparative analysis of disability laws in the United States to the United Nations Convention on the Rights of Persons with Disabilities, 2008', accessed 6 October 2011, http://www.ncd.gov/publications/2008/May122008. The paper provides comprehensive information about the Convention on the Rights of Persons with Disabilities, analysing whether, if ratified by the United States, the Convention might impact U.S. disability law by examining the degree to which U.S. law is consistent with the CRPD.

[6] All articles of the UN CRPD can be accessed on the UN Web site, http://www.un.org/disabilities/convention/conventionfull.shtml.

Article 2 provides the definitions of principal terms including: communication, language, discrimination, reasonable accommodation and universal design.

Article 3 includes guiding principles that are common in international law. There are eight guiding principles: (1) respect for inherent dignity, individual autonomy including the freedom to make one's own choices, and independence of persons; (2) non-discrimination; (3) full and effective participation and inclusion in society; (4) respect for difference and acceptance of persons with disabilities as part of human diversity and humanity; (5) equality of opportunity; (6) accessibility; (7) equality between men and women; and (8) respect for the evolving capacities of children with disabilities and respect for the right of children with disabilities to preserve their identities.

STRUCTURE, CONTENT, SIGNATURE AND RATIFYING

In addition to Articles 1 through 3, which set out the purpose, definitions and principles of CRPD, the Convention has an additional fifty-six articles. Article 4 is basically a continuation of Article 3 and instructs states parties to consult and involve people with disabilities and their representative organisations in the development and implementation of legislation and policies in implementing the CRPD. Article 4 also addresses states parties as to the implementation of economic, social and cultural rights provisions.[7]

Article 5 addresses equality and non-discrimination on the basis of disability, when read in conjunction with the definition of *discrimination on the basis of disability* in Article 2. It prohibits discrimination related to disability, regardless of whether the person discriminated against self-identifies as, or is considered by others to be, a person with disability.

Articles 6 and 7 shed light on two separate populations that experience special discrimination: women and children, the latter being associated with Article 23 of the Convention on the Rights of the Child. Articles 8 and 9 deal with societal barriers to the full and effective inclusion of people with disabilities in societies, specifically attitudinal, physical, informational and communication barriers. Article 8 applies directly to

---

[7] Ibid.

social exclusion, calling on states parties to engage in awareness-raising measures to combat stereotypes, prejudices and harmful practices, and to promote respect for the human rights of people with disabilities. Article 9 explores accessibility issues such as transportation, navigation and accommodation and information dissemination, and so on.[8]

Articles 10 through 30 address a wide variety of human rights issues.[9] They call to abandon traditional medical and social welfare policies and replace them with civil, political, economic, social and cultural rights. Article 12 demonstrates the call for abandoning the traditional domestic approach of denying legal capacity to people with disabilities. The ad hoc committee agreed to adopt Article 12 with the understanding that failure to recognise the legal capacity of people with disabilities has historically deprived many people with disabilities from full enjoyment of their human rights.

Articles 31 through 40 are similar to those used in international environmental law and are geared toward implementation and monitoring of the CRPD. Article 31 highlights the collection of data and statistics to be used by the states. Article 32 encourages international cooperation and sharing of knowledge and experiences. Article 40 represents the first time that a conference of states parties was established with regard to a UN human rights convention.

Article 33 calls for a national-level monitoring of the implementation of the CRPD. It is expected that national human rights institutions, which by definition under the Paris Principles must be 'independent', will have critical roles to play in achieving the national-level monitoring envisioned in Article 33.[10] Articles 34 through 39 address international-level monitoring by establishing a committee of experts that also includes people with disabilities. The committee will be mandated to consider reports of states parties and to interpret the provisions of the CRPD.

Finally, Articles 41 through 50 address human rights issues such as depository, signature, consent to be bound, entry into force and reservations. Notable is the inclusion of Article 44, which allows 'regional integration organisations' to formally consent to be bound by the CRPD to the extent of their competence.[11]

---

[8] Ibid., Articles 6–9.
[9] Ibid., Articles 10–30.
[10] Ibid., Article 33 and Articles 34–39.
[11] Ibid., Articles 41–50.

With respect to social inclusion conceptualisation, the CRPD is based on the social model of disability that emphasises the responsibility of society to dismantle the physical and attitudinal barriers that exclude and stigmatise people on the basis of their physical or mental condition.[12] As such, the CRPD seeks to limit mechanisms that replicate and reinforce the social exclusion and marginalisation of people with disabilities. To achieve this, it sets out the foundational human rights of non-discrimination, equality and social participation as entitlements that must be constructed in the social fabric.

The CRPD is actually a treaty and is considered an international law human rights instrument. In order for such an instrument to bind a state in international law, a state must first sign the Convention and second, ratify the Convention. Where a state ratifies a human rights convention, it becomes a 'party state' to that convention, and this stage is known as 'ratification'. By ratifying the convention, that (party) state accepts its legal obligations in international law and must make sure it meets certain standards of behaviour. The party state is now under a legal obligation in international law to make sure that the human rights as set out in the Convention are not violated in that party state.

The period between which a state signs and then ratifies a convention is termed a 'ratification process'. This is a period of time during which a state is deciding politically whether to ratify the convention. During this period a state also needs to take measures to prepare to ratify a convention such as checking domestic legislation against the convention it is considering ratifying. The ratification process can take a short period of time or a number of years, depending on a state's legal system and political priorities.

UN CRPD: APPLICATION TO DOMESTIC LAW AND POLICY

The CRPD is the most rapidly negotiated human rights treaty to date, and since its adoption it has received impressive global support. It has

---

[12] Gerard Quinn and Theresia Degener, 'Human rights and disability: The current use and future potential of United Nations human rights instruments in the context of disability' (New York and Geneva: OHCHR, United Nations, 2002).

the potential to become the first human rights treaty of the twenty-first century, as well as the first legally enforceable UN instrument specifically applicable to persons with disabilities.[13] Similar to the rationale of this book – to examine social and legal strategies that promote social inclusion of people with disabilities – the CRPD offers two similar perspectives. The first is protection of rights that prohibit denial of basic rights such as expression of speech, thought, religion and political participation. The second is the provision of adequate standards of living.

There is no doubt that the most important mission of the CRPD is its ability to be translated from declarative and abstract rights to domestic law and policy and concrete results. The challenge of each state is to use inclusive practices that will enable significant transformation of abstract rights to concrete advances and serve as a catalyst for social integration of people with disabilities.[14]

The Convention has to be viewed as a process that has to be implemented gradually. It is clear that the course of the legislative process will differ according to the relevant domestic legal systems. The intention is that the incorporation of international human rights principles and norms in national constitutions will enhance international standards. In this regard, there is a concern that the pressures to ratify and the tendency to retain domestic national laws may compromise both the quality of the process as well as the end result.

The gap between domestic disability laws in the United States and the CRPD is evident.[15] Examining the degree to which U.S. law is consistent with the CRPD, it appears that in general terms the aims of the CRPD are consistent with U.S. disability law. For the majority of articles, U.S. law can be viewed as either being on a level with the mandates of the Convention or capable of reaching those levels either through more rigorous implementation and/or additional actions by Congress. However, the

---

[13] See Michael A. Stein, 'A quick overview of the United Nations convention on the rights of persons with disabilities and its implications for Americans with disabilities', *Mental & Physical Disability Law Reporter* 31 (2007), 679–83.

[14] See Michael A. Stein and Janet E. Lord, 'The United Nations Convention on the Rights of Persons with Disabilities as a vehicle for social transformation', in *National Monitoring Mechanisms of the Convention on the Rights of Persons with Disabilities*, accessed at http://200.33.14.34:1010/novedades/mecanismosNacionales.pdf#page=109.

[15] National Council on Disability, 'Finding the gaps,' pp. 3–6.

comparison also identifies several CRPD articles that illustrate significant gaps between U.S. disability laws and the Convention.

It is important to highlight those articles identified as currently having the most significant gaps between U.S. law and policy and the CRPD as they become targets for discussion and bridging the gaps. There is a gap in Article 5, which considers equality and non-discrimination. Current U.S. law and policy lacks equality measures such as vocational training, affirmative action, quotas and job set-asides. Another gap is in Article 6, related to women with disabilities, as current U.S. law and policy lacks positive measures sufficient to ensure the full and equal enjoyment of all human rights. A gap exists in Article 7 regarding children with disabilities, in that their rights are handled by the states rather than by federal U.S. law. Article 8, which deals with awareness raising, is missing from U.S. law and policy as there is no affirmative mandate to alter social stereotypes. Article 9, which is under the enforcement arm of federal law, creates a gap between legal requirements and reality regarding accessibilty. With respect to Article 11, which addresses situations of risk and humanitarian emergencies, current U.S. laws and policies prohibiting discrimination in the provision of services relating to emergency services have not been implemented. Article 12, which addresses legal capacity, is governed primarily by state-level law. Regarding Article 13, which addresses access to justice, U.S. courts have interpreted physical access to court services to be limited by a fundamental alteration defence and have not sufficiently ensured other access to justice.

Article 16 provides freedom from exploitation, violence and abuse and is absent from current U.S. law and policy; the latter does not provide proactive education and training to prevent exploitation, violence and abuse. Article 18, on liberty of movement and nationality, stands in conflict with current U.S. immigration policy, which restricts potential residents and certain visitors with disabilities. Article 19, on living independently and being included in the community, is different from current U.S. law and policy, which limits the right to live in the community to services that do not cause fundamental alterations.[16]

Article 20, which deals with personal mobility, is partially different as current U.S. law and policy does not recognise a right to the provision

---

[16] UN CRPD: Article 19.

of medical and assistive devices in the manner required by the CRPD. Article 23, on respect for home and the family, is handled by the state rather than by U.S. federal law. Article 24, which addresses education, is slightly different in that current U.S. law does not seek to develop children's full potential but instead requires an adequate education. Article 25, regarding health, is handled by state rather than U.S. federal law. Article 27 addresses work and employment, and is different in the sense that current U.S. law and policy does not provide equality measures such as vocational training, affirmative action or job set-asides. Article 28, on adequate standards of living and social protection, is absent in U.S. law as the latter does not recognise economic or social protections as rights. Article 29, on participation in political and public life, is quite similar except where it relates to voting rights. Article 30, on participation in cultural life, recreation, leisure and sport, is different as current U.S. law does not recognise cultural, recreational, leisure or sport participation as an affirmative right. Finally, Article 32, which addresses international cooperation, is missing altogether from U.S. law, which does not mandate inclusive-development practices abroad.

It is important to emphasise, however, that these gaps are capable of being narrowed or eradicated through more rigorous implementation of existing U.S. laws and policies and/or through congressional action.[17]

The CRPD may have an important role in fighting discrimination and exclusion of people with disabilities in Europe.[18] Jarlath Clifford, who recently examined the impact of the CRPD on European law, highlighted four provisions: consultation and involvement, reasonable accommodation, legal capacity and violence and abuse.[19]

Consultation and involvement respond to the ignorance and misperception of persons with disabilities who are excluded and denied social participation and involvement in decision making in European societies. The CRPD requires consultation and involvement through Article 4(3): 'In the development and implementation of legislation and policies to implement the present Convention, and in other decision-making

---

[17] National Council on Disability 'Finding the gaps', p. 6.

[18] Jarlath Clifford, 'The UN Disability Convention and its impact on European Equality Law', *The Equal Rights Review* 6 (2011), 11–25.

[19] Ibid., 14–17.

processes concerning issues relating to persons with disabilities, States Parties shall closely consult with and actively involve persons with disabilities, including children with disabilities, through their representative organizations'.[20] Article 4(3) of the CRPD calls for these provisions as they can be the starting point for developing legislation and policy to implement the Convention. Such consultation and involvement are crucial for creating laws and policies relating to disability issues.

Reasonable accommodation is a core provision in Article 2 of the CRPD and is defined as 'necessary and appropriate modification and adjustments not imposing a disproportionate or undue burden, where needed in a particular case, to ensure to persons with disabilities the enjoyment or exercise on an equal basis with others of all human rights and fundamental freedoms'.[21]

This definition is more far-reaching than the definition contained in Article 5 of the EU Council Directive 2000/78/EC of 27 November 2000, which, within the context of employment and occupation, requires that: 'Employers shall take appropriate measures, where needed in a particular case, to enable a person with a disability to have access to, participate in, or advance in employment, or to undergo training, unless such measures would impose a disproportionate burden on the employer'.[22] Although many states within the EU believe that they provide reasonable accommodation in employment and occupation, Article 5(3) of the CRPD requests broader requirement. States parties must take all appropriate reasonable accommodation steps to promote equality in the enjoyment and exercise of all human rights by persons with disabilities.

Legal capacity is definitely one of the innovative and unique contributions of the Convention: Article 12 of the CRPD provides that states parties reaffirm that persons with disabilities have the right to recognition everywhere as persons before the law; that they recognise that persons with disabilities enjoy legal capacity on an equal basis with others in all aspects of life; that they take appropriate measures to provide access by persons with disabilities to the support they may require in

---

[20] Ibid., 14.

[21] Ibid., 14–15.

[22] Article 5 Council Directive 2000/78/EC of 27 November 2000 establishing a general framework for equal treatment in employment and occupation. Accessed at http://eur-lex.europa.eu/LexUriServ/LexUriServ.do?uri=CELEX:32000L0078:en:HTML.

exercising their legal capacity; and that they ensure that all measures that relate to the exercise of legal capacity provide for appropriate and effective safeguards to prevent abuse in accordance with international human rights law.

Article 12 of the CRPD has great potential to create positive change in Europe, where many states continue to deny or restrict the legal capacity of persons with intellectual or mental impairment through court action. For example, in cases of severe mental or intellectual impairment, appropriate measures may include electing a personal representative to support the person in taking decisions and exercising their legal capacity.

However, Gerard Quinn raised the concern that, in practice, the term would be interpreted by the state as a restrictive measure, leaning toward exclusion rather than the inclusion of the person. In Quinn's words, 'Incapacity is not really a black and white issue, it is very much an individualised process. The first thing that a political authority should look to do is to put in the supports to enable individuals to make decisions, rather than take away this opportunity and do the easier thing of letting another person make the decision for them'.[23]

The fourth area of the CRPD as a potential provision for change in Europe is Article 16, which calls for preventing violence and abuse toward people with disabilities.[24] The implementation of Article 16 is needed because in several countries there are no laws in place that deal with aggravated offences on the grounds of disability, and it appears that relatively few countries keep records of such crimes.

International and national advocacy groups are concerned about the implacability of the CRPD. The International Disability Alliance (IDA), a central stockholder in the international arena, has suggested a roadmap for full and effective implementation of the CRPD, which will address expected obstacles.[25]

---

[23] See The Equal Rights Trust, 'Interview: Promoting a paradigm shift: ERT talks with Gabor Gombos and Gerard Quinn about the UN CRPD and its optional protocol', *The Equal Rights Review* 2 (2008), 90; accessed at http://www.equalrightstrust.org/ertdocumentbank/err_issue02%20reduced.pdf.

[24] Ibid.

[25] See the International Disability Alliance (IDA) position paper on the UN CRPD and other instruments, accessed 25 April 2008, www.un.org/disabilities/documents/COP/IDA%20CRPD%20paper.doc.

A central obstacle that states have to cope with is consistency between the CRPD and domestic law. There is a need for aligning legislation not only in order to avoid inconsistencies between national laws and the new Convention, but also because many of the provisions of the Convention need more detailed legislation to become fully operational. It has been suggested that the process of systematic revision of legislation needs to include both disability-specific legislation as well as all mainstream legislation that is relevant for persons with disabilities including the existing legislation on education, employment and electoral laws.

The lack of awareness of the rights of people with disabilities is another important obstacle. The response is specified in Article 8 of the CRPD, which mandates states to undertake awareness-raising actions on the rights of persons with disabilities and on the CRPD. The IDA views awareness-raising actions as important for creating tolerance and the right climate for change. Therefore, these activities have to also involve persons with disabilities and their families, and it must be seen to that this is being done with the active involvement of representative organisations of persons with disabilities.

The lack of accessibility at the state level is a major barrier to implementation. The IDA calls for the translation of the Convention into national languages to ensure that all persons are aware of it. Disability advocacy organisations have to be involved and particularly check the disability-specific terminology. CRPD versions in national sign languages need also to be made available at no cost. It is also important that the CRPD is made available in alternative formats, in particular in Braille and in plain language. Beyond translation, it is crucial that states ensure an effective dissemination of the CRPD and related national legislations throughout their countries.

A clear obstacle is the old and current public policies in each state. A systematic revision of all public policies (disability-specific and general) is required by the CRPD. Existing public policies need to be checked to ensure that they are fully accessible to all persons with disabilities, through the provision of reasonable, individualised accommodations and the provision of those support services that will enable persons with disabilities to benefit from mainstream services.

Another problem is the current national budget system and the need for state and local governments to work closely together to prevent flaws in implementation. The IDA recommends checking whether the implementation of the CRPD requires an increased resource allocation. Sometimes this will imply a reallocation of budgets from segregated solutions to inclusive solutions, but it will often mean creating and increasing budget allocations.

The CRPD lacks an agreed and clear definition of disability or persons with disabilities, but establishes a minimum threshold that all national definitions need to meet (Article 1). The IDA has suggested that domestic advocacy groups explain to their governments that, irrespective of their type and level of disability, it is the government's responsibility to protect persons with disabilities from discrimination on the basis of disability. Although it may be reasonable to define certain minimum criteria for access to disability-related benefits, protection from discrimination should not be subject to these same limitations. Additional suggested steps are training and awareness measures targeting specific groups such as employers, trade unions, service providers, judges, health professionals and law enforcement; national accessibility plans/strategies and strengthening of accessibility related legislation; and independent monitoring and improved statistical base.

ARTICLE 19 OF THE UN CRPD: TWO INTERNATIONAL ILLUSTRATIONS RELATED TO SOCIAL INCLUSION

Article 19 of the CRPD, on the right of all people with disabilities to live in the community with choices equal to others, is central to social inclusion. This Article requires states to enable people with disabilities to be fully included and participate in society. Community living refers to people with disabilities being able to live in their local communities as equal citizens with the support that they need to participate in everyday life. This includes living in their own homes or with their families, going to work, going to school and taking part in community activities. To ensure that they have the same choices, control and freedom as other citizens, any practical assistance provided them should be based on their own choices and aspirations.

THE EUROPEAN COALITION FOR COMMUNITY LIVING REPORT (2009): FOCUS ON ARTICLE 19

Article 19 meets a very serious concern about institutionalisation rates in Central and Eastern Europe.[26] There are high numbers of people with intellectual and psychiatric disabilities who live in institutional care and are remote and isolated from their families and communities. There is striking evidence that there are widespread human rights abuses in these institutions, such as the use of physical restraints, sexual and physical abuse by staff and other residents and inadequate food, heating and clothing.

Institutionalisation is by no means exclusive to Central and Eastern Europe. A recent research report of institutionalisation in the EU member states and Turkey found that nearly 1.2 million people with disabilities live in institutions.[27] This is likely to be an underestimate because most countries keep only partial data about the number of people in institutions, and others provided no data to the researchers. The study revealed that in sixteen of twenty-five countries for which information was available, state funds were being used, at least in part, to support more than one hundred institutions. In twenty countries across Europe, state funds were being used to support institutions in more than thirty towns.

It seems that applying Article 19 to European countries that still extensively use institutional care policies is a challenge. A new report that focuses on applying Article 19 pointed out that European states practise social exclusion policies.[28] States that continue to rely on institutions as

---

[26] Chiriacescu, D., *Shifting the paradigm in social service provision: Making quality services accessible for people with disabilities in south-east Europe* (Sarajevo: Handicap International, 2008).

This report presents the situation of social services for people with disabilities in the following South East European countries: Albania, Bosnia and Herzegovina, Croatia, FYR Macedonia, Montenegro, Romania, Serbia and Kosovo. The terms 'region' and 'regional' will refer therefore to these countries/locations.

[27] Jim Mansell et al., *Deinstitutionalisation and community living – outcomes and costs: Report of a European study. Volume 1: Executive summary* (Canterbury: The Tizard Centre, University of Kent, 2007).

[28] The European Coalition for Community Living (ECCL), *Focus report on Article 19 of the UN Convention on the Rights of Persons with Disabilities, 2009*, accessed 22 December 2011, www.mhe-sme.org/assets/files/ECCL-Focus-Report-2009-final-high-res.pdf. This report

the preferred model of care deny Article 19, which explicitly requires that services for people with disabilities should 'support living and inclusion in the community' and aim to 'prevent isolation or segregation from the community'.[29]

Furthermore, the right to live in the community and experience social inclusion is central to the implementation of many other rights in the CRPD. For example, the right to habilitation and rehabilitation (Article 26), which requires that states enable disabled people to attain and maintain maximum independence and the right to work on an equal basis with others (Article 27), cannot be achieved if disabled people are not supported to live in the community.

The report outlines the steps that states have to adopt with respect to Article 19. The first is a clear commitment to the right of all people with disabilities to live in the community. However, as implementation needs time, governments have to take concrete measures toward realising this right, using the maximum of their available resources to do so. This is because the CRPD, although acknowledging that it often takes time to achieve economic, social and cultural rights, requires states to take measures with a view 'to achieving progressively the full realization of these rights'.[30] States should therefore plan what action they will need to take to meet their obligations under Article 19; for many, this will include the planning and development of community-based services as alternatives to institutionalisation.

Article 19 is linked to other articles of the CRPD and therefore cannot be implemented without significant progress in others. For example, there is a clear association between Article 12 (equal recognition before the law), Article 14 (liberty and security of person) and Article 23 (respect for home and the family). The implementation of these articles is dependent on countries' major steps in ensuring the right of disabled people to

---

was prepared by the European Coalition for Community Living (ECCL) as part of its work to promote the right of disabled people to live in the community as equal citizens. It focuses on Article 19 of the UN CRPD. The report seeks to provide a clear explanation of the scope and purpose of Article 19 and makes a series of recommendations designed to facilitate the effective implementation of this right.

[29] Ibid., UN CRPD: Article 19.
[30] Ibid.

choose where and with whom to live, and their ability to participate in the community.

INTERNATIONAL COMMITTEE OF EXPERTS ON ISRAEL'S INSTITUTIONALISATION AND COMMUNITY CARE (2011)

Another demonstration of the importance of Article 19 was evident in the recent International Committee of Experts that was invited in 2011 by the Israeli Ministry of Welfare and Social Affairs (MOLSA) to comment on the rights of people with intellectual disabilities to live in the community.[31] The committee, headed by Arie Rimmerman (Israel), included Gerard Quinn (Ireland), Meindert Haveman (Germany/the Netherlands), Peter Blanck and Joel Levy (United States).

According to MOLSA, there are 35,000 people with intellectual disability (ID) in Israel, 9,493 of which (36 percent) live in out-of-home arrangements. The majority of residents (75 percent) live in medium and large facilities (with at least twenty-five other people), approximately one fifth (18 percent), are housed in medium and small residences (with seven to twenty-four people), and 8.2 percent of residents live in apartments with fewer than six persons.[32]

The committee found that there was an ongoing debate between MOLSA and Bizchut regarding institutionalisation and community-based residential policies and programmes.[33] Bizchut advocates for the closure of all institutions and the downsizing of medium and large community-based residences. MOLSA, and to some degree Akim,[34]

---

[31] International Committee of Experts, *Integrated community living for people with intellectual disabilities in Israel*, final report submitted to the Israeli Ministry of Social Affairs and Social Services, Jerusalem, Israel, 2011.

[32] Reneta Gorbatov et al., *Review of existing services* (Jerusalem, Israel: Ministry of Welfare and Social Affairs, 2010).

[33] Bizchut – the Israeli Human Rights Center for People with Disabilities – is a national advocacy organisation. It was founded in 1992 by the Association for Civil Rights in Israel (ACRI) and shortly thereafter became an independent organisation. Bizchut represents people across the entire spectrum of disabilities, regardless of age, gender, ethnic or religious background.

[34] Akim is a national organisation for adults and parents of children with intellectual disabilities. It was founded in 1951 and serves as both an advocate and service provider.

would like to see a moderate change which includes downsizing but not complete closure of large- and medium-sized facilities.

The different ideologies among the parties involved reflect former legislation concerning persons with ID.[35] The legislation, in a nutshell, is oriented toward out-of-home placements – primarily institutionalisation, rather than community-based services – and therefore reflects a paternalistic and segregated view of persons with ID. While the legislation remained unchanged, the policies and practices were influenced by international trends such as independent living, the normalisation principle, inclusion and the disability rights approaches.

The current residential services reflect a mixed policy of institutionalisation and the development of smaller-scale community-based residential facilities, including group homes. Thus, the current state of affairs in Israel reflects a gap between the original legislation and contemporary policies. However, as long as these policies are still linked to legislation that does not align with community-based services, they are bound to only partially align with contemporary international policies and approaches.

Using a benchmarking perspective, the International Committee of Experts found that in contrast to Israel 75 percent of persons with ID in the United States live in various housing arrangements that host six or fewer individuals.[36] Ten percent of all individuals surveyed lived in residences that housed seven to fifteen individuals, and 15 percent of the population surveyed lived in various institutions, that is, facilities with sixteen residents or more.

In comparison to Israel, the policies in Europe, as discussed earlier,[37] show variance from country to country, although the pattern is clear: The trend is toward community living and deinstitutionalisation. Norway and Sweden have completely closed institutional care, and in the UK the process of deinstitutionalisation is well advanced such that the

---

[35] See, for example, 'The Welfare (Treatment of Persons with Mental Disabilities) Law, 5729–1969'.

[36] David Braddock et al., *The state of the states in developmental disabilities 2011*, Department of Psychiatry and Coleman Institute for Cognitive Disabilities, University of Colorado, Denver, 2011.

[37] European Coalition for Community Living, *Focus report on Article 19 of the UN Convention on the Rights of Persons with Disabilities, 2009*. Access the report at www.mhe-sme.org/assets/files/ECCL-Focus-Report-2009-final-high-res.pdf.

number of large institutions is continually decreasing.[38] In countries such as Belgium, the Netherlands, Germany, Spain, Greece, Italy and Portugal, there are varying types of institutional care even though the number of people in large residential institutions is also decreasing.[39] In countries such as France, Hungary, Poland, Romania and the Czech Republic (and Central and Eastern Europe, in general) large institutional facilities are the predominant mode of care.[40]

In the Republic of Ireland, there is a fast process of downsizing the larger institutions, the so-called congregate settings. Ireland and Israel are similar in population size. A recent survey showed far fewer people with ID in institutions in Ireland than in Israel.[41] In Ireland, approximately 3,800 individuals with ID reside in seventy-two institutions ('congregated settings' with eight residents or more), while in Israel 5,862 individuals live in very large facilities (i.e., that house at least sixty-one people).

The International Committee of Experts on Israel's Institutionalisation and Community Care, has been aware to the above trends. The decision was to pay particular attention to four articles of the Convention: Article 12 (the right to make decisions for oneself); Article 19 (the right to living independently and being included in the community); Article 8 (raising awareness as a social precondition to create openness and tolerance for individual expression); and Article 16 (a new way of balancing the legitimate protective role of the state). Article 19 of the Convention is central, as it does not simply reflect civil rights in isolation, as in U.S. thought, but rather stresses the dynamics between civil rights and social provision.

This article weaves together two core principles: (1) the right of people with disabilities to live independently (and consequently the right to

---

[38] Jim Mansell and Julie Beadle-Brown, 'Deinstitutionalisation and community living: Position statement of the comparative policy and practice special interest research group of the International Association for the Scientific Study of Intellectual Disabilities', *Journal of Intellectual Disability Research* 54 (2010), 104–12.

[39] Mansell and Beadle-Brown, 'Deinstitutionalisation and community living', 104–5.

[40] Geert Freyhoff et al., 'Included in society: Results and recommendations of the European research initiative on community-based residential alternatives for disabled people', Brussels, Inclusion Europe. Access the document at http://inclusion-europe.org/sy/projects/past-projects/included-in-society.

[41] See the Working Group on Congregated Settings in the Republic of Ireland, 'Time to move on from congregated care settings: A strategy for community inclusion', 2011, accessed 4 December 2011, http://www.hse.ie/eng/services/Publications/services/Disability/timetomoveonpdf.html.

choose a place of residence) and (2) the entitlement to be fully integrated into the community. The latter entails that placement without the appropriate services to facilitate involvement of individuals in community life and activities will fail to fulfill the principles of the article.

The International Committee of Experts recommended that, based on Article 19 of the Convention, Israel adopt new legislation and policies based on the rights of people with intellectual disabilities. In this sense, the country will be appropriately following in the footsteps of other Western countries that have adopted the CRPD concerning community-based services with emphasis on inclusion and integration. Guided by the principles of the Convention, persons with ID have to be active partners of the change, which can last up to ten years.[42]

THE STATUS OF THE UN CRPD IN DOMESTIC COURTS

The UN CRPD was signed in 2007, therefore it is still early to examine whether it has been used in domestic courts. However, the current status provides early impressions as recorded in the United States, Europe and Australia.

THE UNITED STATES

The UN CRPD has not been ratified in the United States. Part of U.S. objection is related to the belief that the CRPD cannot replace the constitution and U.S. law. If the United States would ratify the Convention, it is unlikely that it would replace it with current laws. The belief is that the text of the Convention gives no indication that its drafters intended its provisions to be automatically enforceable under the domestic law of the states parties. The U.S. Supreme Court has long recognised the distinction between treaties that automatically have an effect as domestic law and those that – while they constitute international law commitments – do

---

[42] See Preamble (O) of the UN CRPD, 'Considering that persons with disabilities should have the opportunity to be actively involved in decision-making processes about policies and programs, including those directly concerning them; accessed 4 April 2011, http://www2.ohchr .org/english/law/disabilities-convention.htm.

not by themselves function as binding federal law.[43] Therefore, it is unlikely that the United States would adopt provisions that have to be enforced in U.S. courts.

THE EUROPEAN UNION

The European Commission (EC) signed the UN Convention on the Rights of Persons with Disabilities in 2009 and ratified it in December 2010. It is handled as a mixed agreement, namely, part of an international agreement that falls within the scope of EU powers and within the powers of the member states. As such, it is debatable and raises legal challenges as it is interrelated to both EU law and international public law. Many areas of the Convention extend beyond non-discrimination, which has been reflected in the dual legal basis. Moreover, the scope of the Convention is extremely broad and covers civil, political, economic, cultural and social rights.[44]

From an EU law perspective, the UN CRPD has become an integral part of EU law. The UN CRPD is situated formally below the provisions of the treaties. In hierarchical terms, the Convention is *inferior* to the provisions of the Treaty on the Functioning of the EU (and the Treaty on the European Union), but *superior* to secondary EU law.[45]

An illustration demonstrating the application of the UN CRPD is cited in a fairly new ruling on disability at the European Court of Human Rights. In its judgment on *Glor v. Switzerland*,[46] the court held that

---

[43] See *Medellin v. Texas*, 552 U.S. 491, 504 2008. Access www.supremecourt.gov/opinions/07pdf/06-984.pdf. Following the Supreme Court's 2008 decision in *Medellin v. Texas*, the United States' policy is that even when, via ratified treaty, the nation consents to the jurisdiction of international courts to issue binding international decisions, 'not all international law obligations automatically constitute binding federal law enforceable in United States courts'.

[44] Lisa Waddington, 'A new era in human rights protection in the European Community: The implications [of] the United Nations' Convention on the Rights of Persons with Disabilities for the European community', Maastricht Faculty of Law Working Paper No. 2007–4, accessed at SSRN: http://ssrn.com/abstract=1026581.

[45] For comprehensive review of the institutionalisation of human rights in the EU, see Frank Schimmelfennig, 'Competition and community: Constitutional courts, rhetorical action, and the institutionalization of human rights in the European Union', *Journal of European Public Policy* 13 (2006), 1247–64.

[46] Application No. 13444/04, Judgment 30 April 2009.

the Swiss government had violated Sven Glor's rights under Article 14 (prohibition of discrimination) in conjunction with Article 8 (right to private and family life) of the European Convention on Human Rights by levying a tax for exemption from military service. He was a person who, because of his disabilities, could not carry out compulsory military service.

Glor was deemed medically unfit to perform military service due to diabetes. His condition, according to the Swiss authorities, posed a problem on account of the particular restrictions related to military service that included limited access to medical care and medication, significant physical efforts required and psychological pressure exerted. However, the authorities decided that Glor's diabetes was not severe enough to relieve him from paying a non-negligible military service exemption tax on his annual earnings for several years to come.

Glor, however, wanted to carry out his military service, but was prohibited from doing so. In addition, he was not permitted to carry out alternative civil service, which was only available to conscientious objectors. Invoking Article 14 together with Article 8 of the European Convention on Human Rights, Glor argued that he had been subjected to discrimination on the basis of his disability because he had been prohibited from carrying out his military service and was obliged to pay the exemption tax, as his disability was judged not to be severe enough for him to forgo the tax.

This is the first ever ruling by the European Court of Human Rights in which the court has found a violation of Article 14 on the grounds of disability. Article 14 prohibits discrimination on any grounds in relation to the rights and freedom set forth in this Convention. In its judgment, the court reiterated that Article 14 contains a non-exhaustive list of prohibited grounds, which also encompasses discrimination based on disability.

In examining the arguments of the parties, the European Court of Human Rights found that the Swiss authorities did not fairly weigh the interests of society against Glor's human rights. In particular, the court concluded that no objective justification existed in a democratic society to distinguish between persons with disabilities who are exempt from the tax and persons with disabilities who are obliged to pay the tax.

In addition, this judgment condemned the Swiss authorities for failing to provide reasonable accommodation in finding a solution which responded to Glor's individual circumstances, echoing Article 2 of the UN CRPD, which defines reasonable accommodation as the 'necessary and appropriate modification and adjustments not imposing a disproportionate or undue burden, where needed in a particular case, to ensure to persons with disabilities the enjoyment or exercise on an equal basis with others of all human rights and fundamental freedoms the Court calls for the implementation of reasonable accommodation'.[47] A fairly good example is filling posts in the armed forces that require less physical effort by persons with disabilities. In highlighting the failure of the Swiss authorities, the court pointed to legislation in other countries that ensures the recruitment of persons with disabilities to posts that have been adapted to both the person's disability and to the person's set of professional skills.

It is one of the first cases in which the court makes explicit reference to the UN CRPD as the basis for the existence of a European and universal consensus on the need to protect persons with disabilities from discriminatory treatment. It does so despite the fact that Switzerland has not yet signed the disability-specific Convention, indicating that the court values the Convention as an up-to-date and universal consensus on the need to protect people with disabilities against all forms of discrimination.

AUSTRALIA

The UN CRPD has been cited in court and tribunal decisions in Australia.[48] However, the use of the Convention in court decisions has been viewed as a marginal citation.[49]

The most interesting example of utilising the Convention was the Supreme Court ruling in the case of *Vickery J. v. Betty Dyke* (known as

---

[47] Ibid.

[48] See *Devers v. Kindilan Society* [2009] FCA 1392-Unreported, Marshall J, 27 November 2009); *Halsbury v. Halsbury* (stay application) [2009] FamCAFC 142 (11 August 2009) (unreported); *Kracke v. Mental Health Review Board* [2009] VCAT 646 (Unreported, Bell P, 23 April 2009); *Sales v. Minister for Immigration & Citizenship* (2007) 99 ALD 523; [2007] FCA 2094 (21 December 2007); *Secretary, Department of Families, Housing, Community Services and Indigenous Affairs v. Jansen* (2008) 166 FCR 428; [2008] FCAFC 48 (4 April 2008).

[49] See, for example, Roland McCallum, 'The United Nations Convention on the Rights of Persons with Disabilities: Some reflections' (3 March 2010). Sydney Law School Research Paper No. 10/30, accessed at SSRN: http://ssrn.com/abstract=1563883.

Julie Ann Nicholson v. Timothy Peter Knaggs). Betty Dyke died in 2004 at age eighty-four.[50] She had two major disabilities (physical and cognitive) that increased in severity as she grew older. She received schooling up to grade eight, had never married and had no children. She lived alone on semi-rural property on Victoria's Mornington Peninsula, and as she aged was in acute and constant pain caused by curvature of the spine. She later developed dementia caused by the onset of Alzheimer's disease.

There were a series of wills – the earliest was made in 1985, but two wills were later made in 1999 and 2001. While the 1999 and 2001 wills gave various extended family members and charities small gifts, the bulk of the large estate went to three married couples who were her neighbours (one of the couples was Mr. and Ms. Knaggs). Extended family members and a number of charities who received most of the estate under the 1985 will challenged the 1999 and 2001 wills. The argument by the challengers was that Betty Dyke either lacked the testamentary capacity to make these wills or that when executing the wills she was subjected to undue influence by one of the three sets of married neighbours.

This case is important in the present context because the judge discussed the CRPD and used Article 12 to broaden the Common Law test for testamentary incapacity due to undue influence. After citing the CRPD, the judge endorsed Article 12 and the concept that people with disabilities should have the capacity to exercise legal rights on an equal basis with others in all aspects of life. The article is therefore capable of being applied to the making of wills by persons with disabilities.

The effect of Article 12(2) in the present context is to provide an obligation for Australia to recognise that persons with disabilities enjoy the exercise of the right to freedom of testamentary disposition on an equal basis with all other persons. Undue influence in the will-making process may impose a significant barrier to the free expression of the testator's preferences. Persons with disabilities, including the elderly who suffer from disabilities, are uniquely vulnerable to the exercise of undue influence on the part of others. Accordingly, the common law protection provided by the concept of undue influence, as it has developed in Australia, may legitimately be engaged by the CRPD.

---

[50] *Julie Ann Nicholson & Ors v. Timothy. Peter Knaggs & Ors* [2009] VSC 64.

CONCLUSION

This chapter introduced and reviewed the CRPD, the first human rights treaty of the twenty-first century. It is a comprehensive international instrument based on the social model of disability, and it aims to protect rights of people with disabilities and ensure their social inclusion and full participation. The Convention applies the principle of discrimination to every human right. Therefore, it does not seek to create new rights for disabled persons, but rather elaborates and clarifies existing human rights obligations within the disability context. In terms of structure, the CRPD has two layers. The first layer is protection of rights that prohibit denial of basic rights such as expression of speech, thought, religion and political participation. The second layer is the provision of adequate standards of living.

However, the most important challenge of the CRPD is whether it can be translated from declarative and abstract rights to domestic law, policy and concrete results. This chapter examined the potential transference of CRPD to domestic policy, legislation and domestic courts. Two illustrations from Europe and Israel demonstrate the merit of Article 19 in examining institutionalisation and community-based programmes. It is still early to examine whether it has been adopted in domestic courts. However, examples from U.S., EU and Australian courts reflect that it is relevant but as yet hardly used.

8 STRATEGIES FOR CHANGING MEDIA STEREOTYPES AND BRIDGING DIGITAL DIVIDES

This chapter introduces and analyses national and international strategies to change media stereotypes of people with disabilities. In the second part of the chapter, it will present and discuss arguably the most successful efforts at bridging the digital divide.

STRATEGIES FOR CHANGING STEREOTYPES OF PEOPLE WITH DISABILITIES

Chapter 4 introduces the ambivalent and often distorted portrayal of people with disabilities in the printed and digital media. The conclusion is that writers, editors, directors, producers, filmmakers and advertisers have unintentionally marginalised the appearance of people with disabilities in order to appeal to public stereotypes. In general, there are two core approaches to handling change in media stereotypes. The first approach believes that the media needs guidelines that will prevent biased and negative images of people with disabilities.[1] The second approach is to use the media as a socialisation agent and as a tool for attitudinal change.[2]

Charles Riley, a veteran journalist, is optimistic about the ability to change attitudes toward people with disabilities by depicting disability

---

[1] See, for example, 'Guidelines for reporting and writing about people with disabilities', University of Kansas: Research and Training Center on Independent Living, 2008, 7th edition; Joan Hume, *Media guidelines* (Sydney: Disability Council of New South Wales, 1994).

[2] Charles A. Riley, *Disability and the media: Prescriptions for change* (Lebanon, NH: University Press of New England, 2005), pp. 157–218.

more accurately across all types of media.[3] In his opinion, the solution is in a fair and balanced journalism and the adoption of 'Guidelines for Portraying People with Disabilities in the Media' and 'Guidelines for Web Accessibility'.[4]

However, researchers are more sceptical about the ability to change stereotypes by forming new guidelines. A comprehensive study that examined the required changes in the British Broadcasting Corporation, the Broadcasting Standards Commission and the Independent Television Commission, showed that the solutions are fairly complicated.[5] There is agreement that current images of people with disabilities have to change toward more acceptance and social inclusion. However, there are sub-populations that are still quite biased toward people with disabilities. The research identified 'followers' and 'traditionalist' groups as the most resistant to change in representation. They express lack of interest in people with disabilities and their presentation on television. In order to change the status quo, the media has to overcome these attitudinal barriers and challenge these subpopulations.

Specifically, the first barrier is cultural conditioning, which relates to society's obsession with physical attractiveness. Professionals tend to believe that viewers expect actors and presenters on television to be good looking. There are only one or two professionals who fell into the 'traditionalist' and 'followers' categories. This small sample of broadcasting professionals is reluctant to admit it but often says that people with disabilities can make for uncomfortable viewing.[6]

The second barrier is related to the notion that when people are confronted by something other than themselves, their initial response is one of discomfort and rejection. Therefore, it is important to reduce the sense of 'difference' between people with and without disabilities in order to facilitate acceptance.

---

[3] Ibid., Preface ix–xviii.

[4] Ibid., 219–29.

[5] Jane Sancho, *Disabling prejudice: Attitudes towards disability and its portrayal on television,* report by the British Broadcasting Corporation, the Broadcasting Standards Commission and the Independent Television Commission. Accessed 2 December 2011, downloads.bbc.co.uk/guidelines/editorialguidelines/ . . . /disabling-prejudice.pdf.

[6] Ibid.

The British report offers five triggers that may increase acceptance of people with disability in TV programmes: (1) *matching* – demonstrating the message that people with disabilities are like us ('you are like me'); (2) *likeability* – creating an emotional touch by engaging personality, achievement and sense of humour; (3) *celebrity* – using a famous actor or well-respected figure to play the role of a person with a disability (some consider as old-fashioned and too simplistic); (4) *incidental inclusion* – a person with a disability featuring a person rather than the disability per se; (5) *brief educational/information piece* – widely used to present an educational or information piece to tackle a particular issue.

A thorough review of common strategies of change in portrayals of disability in the media indicates that there is no single preferable approach.[7] There are, clearly, three macro strategies that have been used in the last decade. The first is the European Declaration on Media and Disability adopted during the European Year of People with Disabilities in 2003.[8] The second is Article 8 of the UN CRPD, geared to raise awareness toward disability issues, and the third is the use of Guidelines for Presenting People with Disabilities in the Media.[9] These strategies are widely used in large-scale campaigns in the United States, Europe and Australia. Micro-strategies are based on specific projects that promote change in the media. The most recognised one is the educational U.S. TV programme *The Kids on the Block*.

MACRO STRATEGIES: THE EUROPEAN DECLARATION ON ART, CULTURE, MEDIA AND DISABILITY (2003) AND THE UN CONVENTION ON THE RIGHTS OF PEOPLE WITH DISABILITY (2006)

The Athens declaration on *Media and Disability* called for a change in the way people with disabilities are represented in the media. The

[7] Ibid.

[8] The First European Declaration on Media and Disability of 2003 can be accessed at http://www.edf-feph.org/page_generale.asp?docid=14476. It was presented in Athens at a two-day European Congress,14–16 June 2003. The document provides general guidelines for further action and reflection on how to improve the image of disability in media and advertising, as well as active participation of disabled professionals in this sector.

[9] Ibid.

declaration is an important document that targets the change required in the media sector. It is actually a roadmap calling for cooperation with disability stock holders. Furthermore, the declaration recommended that the media industry hire people with disability and improve their accessibility.[10]

The declaration was very specific about the direction needed to promote inclusion and diversity of people with disability within media organisations; the delivery of disability equality training for employees within the organisations; the encouragement of further education establishments to include disability as a topic within media and communication studies courses; the exchange of best practice within the sector and encouragement of monitoring of progress; the development of training and employment programmes where appropriate to increase the participation of disabled people within the sector; the access audits of workplaces in the media industry; and the development and use of appropriate technologies to promote access for and inclusion of disabled people in media services. The expectation was that a committee would be set up by the European Disability Forum in cooperation with European and national media and advertising organisations.

It is too early to determine whether the declaration has made an impact on the role of people with disabilities in the European media. The impression is that it is recognised by European countries and often cited in current media and disability campaigns.

ARTICLE 8 OF THE UN CONVENTION ON THE RIGHTS OF PEOPLE WITH DISABILITY (2006)

Articles 8 and 9 of the CRPD highlight issues around a number of societal barriers – specifically attitudinal, physical, informational and communication barriers – to the full and effective inclusion of people with disabilities in societies.[11] Article 8 obligates states parties to engage in awareness-raising measures, especially with regard to combating

---

[10] The First European Declaration on Media and Disability of 2003.
[11] UN CRPD.

stereotypes, prejudices and harmful practices, and promoting respect for the human rights of people with disabilities:

1. States parties undertake to adopt immediate, effective and appropriate measures:
   (a) To raise awareness throughout society, including at the family level, regarding persons with disabilities, and to foster respect for the rights and dignity of persons with disabilities;
   (b) To combat stereotypes, prejudices and harmful practices relating to persons with disabilities, including those based on sex and age, in all areas of life;
   (c) To promote awareness of the capabilities and contributions of persons with disabilities.
2. Measures to this end include:
   (a) Initiating and maintaining effective public awareness campaigns designed:
      i. To nurture receptiveness to the rights of persons with disabilities;
      ii. To promote positive perceptions and greater social awareness toward persons with disabilities;
      iii. To promote recognition of the skills, merits and abilities of persons with disabilities, and of their contributions to the workplace and the labour market;
   (b) Fostering at all levels of the education system, including in all children from an early age, an attitude of respect for the rights of persons with disabilities;
   (c) Encouraging all organs of the media to portray persons with disabilities in a manner consistent with the purpose of the present Convention;
   (d) Promoting awareness-training programmes regarding persons with disabilities and the rights of persons with disabilities:
      i. Encouraging all organs of the media to portray persons with disabilities in a manner consistent with the purpose of the present Convention;
      ii. Promoting awareness training programmes regarding persons with disabilities and their rights.[12]

[12] Ibid.

Article 8 was included in the Convention in part to try to address the prevailing attitudes toward persons with disabilities in many states. Prejudice and stereotypes often hindered the adoption of progressive disability rights legislation in some states. Article 8 is viewed as the first international tool that highlights four important steps that governments and other public bodies should take to bring about a culture change, including the need to promote disability equality training.[13] This can be achieved by promoting training for policy and decision makers (local and national), so that they know how to respect, protect and promote the human rights of disabled people so that they can reach their potential in society and have their contributions valued.

However, the most difficult effort is implementation in each country. In response to Article 8, each country will need to ensure that all relevant stakeholders, including persons with disabilities, have adequate information on the rights resulting from the CRPD. The countries have to undertake information campaigns targeting persons with disabilities and informing them about their rights under the CRPD and they will need to support awareness-raising campaigns. The countries will need to ensure that these important campaigns will involve representative organisations of persons with disabilities.

Implementation of Article 8 is almost impossible in the United States because the federal government deregulated the broadcasting industry in the 1980s. Therefore, the CRPD cannot replace the variety of sources, including the existing Advertising (Ad) Council, a nonprofit entity that distributes the majority of produced public service announcements. In addition, the Individuals with Disabilities Education Act (IDEA) requires public schools to make available to all eligible children with disabilities a free, appropriate public education in the least restrictive environment appropriate to their individual needs; however, it does not affirmatively mandate the breakdown of social stigma related to children with disabilities.

---

[13] Katherine Guernsey, Marco Nicoli and Alberto Ninio, 'Convention on the rights of persons with disabilities: Its implementation and relevance for the World Bank', Discussion Paper 0712 (Washington, D.C., The World Bank June 2007). This discussion paper is a World Bank organisational learning tool designed to provide a review and commentary on the relevance of the UN CRPD. Accessed 25 December 2011 at www.consumersunion. org/pdf/telecom1-0299.pdf; http://siteresources.worldbank.org/SOCIALPROTECTION/Resources/SP-Discussion-papers/Disability-DP/0712.pdf.

EUROPEAN AND AUSTRALIAN MEDIA PROJECTS: INCREASING AND IMPROVING THE PORTRAYAL OF PEOPLE WITH DISABILITIES IN THE MEDIA

One of the best ways to examine whether media can change portrayals of people with disabilities is by examining innovative national projects. One such challenging project studied nine European countries: Denmark, Germany, Hungary, Italy, Poland, Slovenia, Spain, Sweden and the UK.[14] The project, coordinated by Spain, included the following organisations: ABM Germany, a nonprofit organisation that operated in the German media for more than twenty years with the aim of increasing the awareness of disability in the public; The Consiglio Nazionale sulla Disabilità (CND) Italy, a unitary and independent Italian body representing persons with disabilities and their families in European actions and policies; MEOSZ Hungary, the national federation of disabled persons associations in Hungary founded by grassroots associations of people with disabilities; HSO Sweden, the Swedish Disability Federation of the Swedish disability movement; TV-GLAD Denmark, the first TV station in the world dedicated to and operated by people with learning disabilities; Fundación ONCE in Spain, the largest cross-disability organisation; the European Association of Communications Agencies (EACA), which brings together advertising, media and sales promotions agencies across Europe, enabling international experience and issues to be shared and dealt with on a pan-European basis; RNIB, the UK's largest disability organisation offering information, support and advice to people with sight problems; Stowaryszenie Przviaciol Integracii (Friends of Integration Association), a Polish non-governmental, nonprofit organisation that provides education and information for people with disabilities; Servimedia in Spain, which was established by Fundación ONCE in 1989 with the aim of promoting social information, including information about people with disabilities, in the mainstream media; NSIOS in Slovenia, the National Council of Disabled People's Organisations which unites fifteen existing Slovenian representative disabled people's organisations.

---

[14] The project was coordinated by Fundación ONCE in 2006 and 2007 in partnership with twelve organisations. Information about the project can be accessed at http://www .mediaanddisability.org/.

The project outcome was the detailed *Guide on Media & Disability*, which can be used as a training tool and road map for media experts.[15] The guide was written by the Broadcasting and Creative Industries Disability Network (BCIDN), a London-based organisation. It is derived from the collective experience of the network and its members who have been working together to try to improve the situation of disabled people in broadcasting, film and advertising over the past decade. The guide is intended for all broadcasters and producers, including those who work in mainstream programme areas from news to light entertainment and from drama to documentaries. It is not just for programme producers working on specialist disability output. Some of the guide is also relevant to commissioning editors, human resource managers, technical staff and staff working directly with listeners and viewers.

The online training tool was constructed by member organisations in 2006 and is available on the project's Web site. This training targets NGOs and is based on the need for disability NGOs to be aware of the objectives to be achieved and of the argumentation to be used when dealing with the mainstream audiovisual industry. The tool covers the following areas: the history of attitudes toward disabled people; the stereotypes of disability common in the moving image; media guidance on avoiding stereotypes; and how to and how not to portray disabled people on television.

It is impossible to present the action plans of all nine countries, so I will present the plans of just three: Germany, the UK and Sweden. The German action plan includes awareness-raising seminars organised by ABM, the German organization for advancement of disabled people in the media. The first seminar offered the NGO's insightful view into the workings of editorial departments (for regional and local news and TV drama) of TV broadcasters, their needs and their ways of thinking. The second seminar demonstrated participants' best practice of inclusion of people with disabilities in mainstream TV and their importance. Both seminars encouraged cooperation between governmental and public media agencies.

The UK's action plan has been pragmatic and based on organised meetings. RNIB has initiated a number of meetings of different stakeholders in the media industry, including the media unions and the Institute

---

[15] Ibid.

of Practitioners in Advertising. One of the highlights, *Make it Happen . . . in the Media,* was a planned event aimed at promoting careers in the media to young students and graduates with disabilities. Workshops were held on careers in television, film, advertising and journalism. As a result of this event, three beneficiaries have started contributing regularly to BBC's Ouch!, the most popular disability Web site in the UK, whereas another beneficiary was hired by the magazine *Disability Now.* An additional RNIB activity was media training for disability NGOs to provide employment specialists from those NGOs with training to more effectively deal with the media.

The Swedish action plan is based on a national seminar carried out by HSO. The organisation was successful in writing cooperation agreements with two out of three public service broadcasting companies, including action points for 2008. Other proposed activities were specific projects such as digital storytelling, through which people with disabilities learn about media by producing short personal stories. The resulting films are distributed through the project 'Room for storytelling' at UR, the Swedish Educational Broadcasting company Web site. Other activities include media training for disability organisations and disability in advertising in which a group of students at the most important school for advertising in Sweden worked with a project on the portrayal of persons with disabilities in advertising from January to May in 2007.

AUSTRALIA'S POSITIVE IMAGE STRATEGY

Australia is probably one of the first countries to respond to Article 8 (raising awareness) of the CRPD. The government adopted a community education project involving media groups to promote positive images of people with disabilities. The campaign, entitled "Future Directions: Towards Challenge 2014," was a government initiative launched in 2010 to create partnerships with media groups, adult education providers and arts groups to promote positive images of people with disabilities and to challenge community attitudes about people with disabilities.[16] The

---

[16] Information about the campaign can be accessed at www.dhcs.act.gov.au/__data/.../final_ policy_framework_PUBLISHED.pdf.

campaign was committed to investigating the development of disability awareness training for universal services, generally for community members, bus drivers, employers and government employees.

The strategy included the following steps: running public awareness campaigns that showcased the positive contributions of people with disabilities; encouraging the media to show what people with disabilities can do; using the education system to teach people to respect and value people with disabilities and promoting awareness educational training about disability.

The interim report released after the first year outlined the campaign's progress. With respect to encouraging the media, it showed that the media, through newspapers, radio, television and advertising, has a significant influence in shaping the community's perceptions and attitudes. People's direct experience, combined with what they see, read and listen to, shapes the way they think and feel about people with disabilities.

The media consisted of professionals gathered to dispense news and stories that provide invaluable opportunities to focus on social problems such as discrimination and access and commentary about possible solutions to address these issues. A variety of national social media was devoted to celebrating, portraying and supporting people with disabilities. An outstanding example was Link Disability Magazine,[17] which features opinions and perspectives from people with disabilities, covering a diverse range of topics including news, issues, art, sport, travel, health, advocacy, products and people in the disability sector. An additional Web site was created in a partnership between the federal government and the Australian Broadcasting Corporation (ABC) to raise awareness of people with disabilities and disability issues.[18] It is developed and edited by people with a disability and provides them with a national voice.

The Australian national campaign also includes a positive change in words and images of people with disabilities, emphasising the value of the lives of people with disabilities, their dignity and strengths, and their continuous contributions to their communities. Finally, an additional component based on research of attitudinal change includes educating

---

[17] See www.linkonline.com.au.
[18] See www.abc.net.au/disability.

youth about respecting people and the provision of disability awareness training that includes contact with people with disabilities.

THE USE OF GUIDELINES FOR DEPICTING PEOPLE WITH DISABILITIES IN THE MEDIA

In recent years, numerous organisations have adopted new guidelines for reporting and presenting disability in the media. The International Labor Organization (ILO) has published a booklet on *Media Guidelines for the Portrayal of Disability* (2010).[19] Another booklet with guidelines was published recently by the Research and Training Center on Independent Living, University of Kansas.[20] The guidelines that are widely used in the United States use recommended preferred terminology and offer suggestions for accurate ways to describe people with disabilities in the printed media. The University of Kansas booklet reflects input from more than one hundred national disability organisations and was reviewed and endorsed by media and disability experts throughout the country.

Portions of the ILO's *Guidelines*, which was originally funded by the National Institute on Disability and Rehabilitation Research, were adopted into the *Associated Press Stylebook*, a basic reference for professional journalists.[21] The first part of the booklet offers tips about unbiased reporting and avoiding stereotyping people with disabilities. The most common suggestions are: not to focus on disability unless it is crucial to the story; to put people first, not their disability; not to portray successful people with disabilities as heroic overachievers or long-suffering saints; to avoid sensationalising and negative labelling; to emphasise abilities, not limitations; and to bypass condescending euphemisms.

The second part of the booklet includes consensus-preferred terms for referring to disabilities. For example, the guide demonstrates the

---

[19] See *Media guidelines for the portrayal of disability* (Geneva: ILO, 2010). Access at www.ilo. org/wcmsp5/groups/public/@ed_emp/.../wcms_127002.pdf.

[20] *Guidelines for reporting and writing about people with disabilities*, 7th edition (Lawrence, KS: University of Kansas, 2008).

[21] The *Associated Press Stylebook*, usually called the *AP Stylebook*, is a style and usage guide used by newspapers and in the news industry in the United States. The book is updated annually by Associated Press editors.

proper use of the term *disability*. It is a general term used for an attribute or functional limitation that interferes with a person's ability – for example, the ability to walk, lift or learn. It may refer to a physical, sensory or mental condition such as Lyme disease, depression, irritable bowel syndrome, post-traumatic stress disorder, diabetes, multiple sclerosis and other conditions that restrict the activities of daily living. There is an instruction not to refer to people with disabilities as *the handicapped* or *handicapped persons* because *disability* and *handicap* are not interchangeable. The guide indicates that *handicap* is an archaic word, originally associated with a disadvantage and today indicates a barrier or source of limitation. Another suggestion is to avoid using *the disabled* as a generic label because it has connotations of non-functioning (for example, *disabled* car); describes a condition and people are not conditions; and implies a homogenous group apart from the rest of society.[22]

MICRO-STRATEGIES TO PROMOTE MEDIA CHANGE TOWARD PEOPLE WITH DISABILITIES

The best-known documented programme to raise children's awareness of disabilities is the U.S. educational programme *The Kids on the Block*.[23] Numerous studies have been conducted to determine how effective this programme has been for young audiences regarding raising awareness of differences, disabilities and social issues.[24] The studies range from informal questionnaires and evaluations to formal research studies conducted by trained researchers. Three different studies that have

---

[22] *Guidelines for reporting and writing about people with disabilities*, 6.

[23] *The Kids on the Block* is an educational puppet troupe that travels to elementary schools across Western New York promoting disability awareness and the acceptance of differences. The program was established in 1977 in direct response to Public Law 94–142, also called the 'mainstreaming law', which required that children with disabilities be educated in the least restrictive environment possible. The puppets were designed to create a comfortable environment that would allow children to openly discuss their questions or concerns. During their performances, myths and misperceptions were replaced with facts and sensitivity.

[24] Shalom M. Fisch, *Children's learning from educational television: Sesame Street and beyond* (Mahwah, NJ: Lawrence Erlbaum Associates, 2004).

demonstrated the merit of this educational programme on children without disabilities are presented in the following paragraphs.

Sarah Gaddy Hawkins' doctoral dissertation studied fifth and sixth grade students from public schools in Northern Virginia who viewed *The Kids on the Block* segments on blindness, mental retardation, learning disabilities, emotional disorders and cerebral palsy.[25] They participated in approximately five hours of follow-up activities (role-playing, disability simulation, etc.) developed by *The Kids on the Block*. Before and after being exposed to the programme, students completed tests designed to determine a change in attitude. Additionally, the researchers administered a follow-up test four weeks after the segments were viewed to determine if *The Kids on the Block* programme had produced lasting attitudinal changes. Findings demonstrated that *The Kids on the Block* puppet programme was a successful method for instilling positive attitudes toward students with and without disabilities. Participating in this media intervention project positively affected attitudes toward disability that have been maintained over time.

Another research study examined changes in knowledge and attitudes, both before and after a scheduled *The Kids on the Block* puppet performance in selected third-grade classrooms in Edmonton, Alberta, Canada.[26] The findings showed a significant increase in factual knowledge, with seventeen out of twenty-five knowledge-based questions having statistically different responses post-test. The children's attitudes were more positive following the puppet presentation. The results strongly suggest that an educational system such *The Kids on the Block* may represent an effective medium through which young children can learn about disabilities and perhaps develop more positive feelings about their peers who are disabled.

A large-scale research study evaluating the impact of *The Kids on the Block* was conducted on the knowledge and attitudes toward individuals

---

[25] Sarah Gaddy Hawkins, *A study of an effort to modify non-handicapped students' attitudes toward the handicapped*, Ph.D. thesis, The College of William and Mary, Williamsburg, Virginia, May 1985.

[26] Fern Snart, 'Examining the effectiveness of one innovative program with the goal to improve the knowledge and attitudes of elementary school aged students toward the disabled using *The Kids on the Block* puppet approach' (Alberta, Canada: University of Alberta, Edmonton, 1993).

with disabilities held by second- and fifth-grade children from thirteen schools in a large mid-western city in Nebraska.[27] The results indicated that students who had watched the programme (the experimental group), expressed significant improvement in their knowledge about disability and their social distance from those with disabilities at post-test and follow-up compared to the control group.

PROGRESSIVE ADVERTISING

Advertising companies prefer bodily perfection and the exclusion of people with disabilities from publicity images. There are at least two ways in which the advertising industry contributes to discrimination. First, people with disabilities are often ignored by mainstream advertisers and advertising agencies. Besides hiding disability from the general public, this is a denial of the role of people with disabilities as citizens and consumers. Second, some advertisers, notably charities, often present a distorted image of disability and people with disabilities in order to raise money. In both cases the people with disabilities are the losers.[28]

There is often tension between advertising companies and disability advocates who are critical about the roles they depict.[29] They feel

---

[27] Jean Marie Schumacher, *The effectiveness of The Kids on the Block program in increasing children's knowledge of and attitudes toward individuals with disabilities* (Omaha: The University of Nebraska at Omaha, 1997).

[28] See two important articles by Beth Haller, 'Profitability, diversity, and disability images in advertising in the United States and Great Britain', *Disability Studies Quarterly* 21 (2001), accessed, http://dsq-sds.org/article/view/276/301 and 'Are disability images in advertising becoming bold and daring? An analysis of prominent themes in US and UK campaigns', *Disability Studies Quarterly* 26 (2006), accessed, http://dsq-sds.org/article/view/716/893; and a UK study by Caroline B. Eayrs and Nick Ellis, 'Charity advertising: For or against people with a mental handicap?' *British Journal of Social Psychology* 29 (1990), 349–66. Their research examines whether it is possible for charity advertising campaigns to stimulate donations successfully as well as represent people with disabilities as valued human beings. The researchers examined attitudes toward MENCAP posters along fifteen bipolar constructs. Findings suggest that images that elicit the greatest commitment to give money are those most closely associated with feelings of guilt, sympathy and pity and are negatively associated with posters which illustrate people with a mental handicap as having the same rights, value and capability as non-handicapped persons.

[29] Lorraine Thomas, 'Disability is not so beautiful: A semiotic analysis of advertisements for rehabilitation goods', *Disability Studies Quarterly* 21 (2001). Accessed, http://dsq-sds.org/article/view/280/309.

that many charities continue to exploit people with disabilities, whereas others focus on the 'courage and bravery' of individual 'super cripples'. Besides emphasising the abnormality of the individuals concerned, this approach reinforces the perceived inadequacy of the rest of the disabled population.

There is an impression that charity advertisers are more aware of their important roles in portraying disability. They tend to focus on the 'abilities' rather than the 'disabilities' and offer progressive advertising that respects diversity of disability and portrays varied experiences. Advertisers have to create dialogue with people with disabilities and involve them in the process and product. By including disabilities in its creative output, advertising will help society gradually come to recognise that disability is a normal and substantial part of the society in which we live.

Progressive advertisement in the disability area intends to raise visibility of people with disabilities, sending a clear message that it is normal to see people with disabilities as our neighbours living in our communities. In addition, the purpose is to acclimatise people with disabilities, illustrating interactions between people with and without disabilities. Finally, it tends to challenge expectations of low capability, focusing on the capabilities and talents of people with disabilities and how they can be integrated into society.

RECOGNITION OF BEST PRACTICE

Recognising successful media practices that have an impact on raising awareness toward people with disabilities is another strategy that promotes change. For example, Leonard Cheshire Disability in the UK, a national charity, awards the Ability Media International (AMI) Award for work from any aspect of the arts, including film, television or radio, which is produced by or presents issues facing people with disabilities.[30] The winner of the AMI award for 2010 in the television drama category was *The Silence*, a compelling thriller about a young deaf girl, played by profoundly deaf actor Genevieve Barr, whose character was thrust into the unfamiliar and uncomfortable hearing world after she underwent a

---

[30] The call can be accessed at http://www.lcdisability.org/?lid=17335.

cochlear implant operation. The result was a challenging drama which handled its provocative themes with sensitivity and responsibility.

A similar annual award, called the Positive Images in the Media Award, is provided by The Association for the Severely Handicapped (TASH) in the United States.[31] This award honours presentations in print, film or other forms of media that promote positive images of people with disabilities in all aspects of community life. Awardees are recognised for their contribution to the elimination of stereotypes by portraying people with disabilities and their lives accurately with recognition of the complexities of being human. The 2010 winner was *New Kind of Listening*, an hour-long documentary that describes the creative work of the Community Inclusive Theatre Group, in which director Richard Reho inspires cast members, some with disabilities, to be writers, actors and dancers in an original collaborative performance.

BRIDGING THE DIGITAL DIVIDE: OVERVIEW OF GENERAL POLICIES

The digital divide has been described as one of the most important areas that people with disabilities have to overcome in order to increase their social participation.[32] Since 2001, more than half of Americans are reported to have Internet access, but despite regular increases over time those with disabilities are not catching up.[33]

Some critics insist that the divide will fade due to market pressures, with decreasing hardware and connectivity costs inevitably levelling the digital playing field.[34] There is some merit to this argument, but only in part. Falling technology costs have indeed allowed more people to

---

[31] Information about TASH's awards can be accessed at http://tash.org/about/award-programs/.

[32] An extensive review of the digital divide is presented in Scott Emery Hollier, 'The disability divide: A study into the impact of computing and internet-related technologies on people who are blind or vision impaired', Cornell University ILR School DigitalCommons@ILR, *GLADNET Collection*. Paper 340, 2007. http://digitalcommons.ilr.cornell.edu/gladnetcollect/340.

[33] For further information, see RTC Rural Facts at 'Disability and the digital divide: Comparing surveys with disability data', June 2006, http://rtc.ruralinstitute.umt.edu/TelCom/Divide.htm.

[34] See, for example, Bharat C. Mehra, Cecelia Merkel and Ann Peterson Bishop, 'The internet for empowerment of minority and marginalized users', *New Media and Society* 6 (2004), 781–802.

participate in the Internet revolution, but the digital divide is not simply an issue of whether everyone can afford access to the Internet.

Most of the national and international solutions for bridging the digital divide are social-techno in nature. The common approach is technological in an attempt to focus almost exclusively on providing access to digital communication technologies, and expects that all the people will benefit from this development. In contrast, social scientists argue that the focus should be on people and their developmental needs, issues of poverty and lack of social-techno access.

One of the common opinions is that the core barriers are access and inequality as those who suffer from economic exclusion online are already disadvantaged offline.[35] The rationale is that inequalities in skills-access translate into inequalities in citizenship skills and marginalisation in terms of civic rights. Therefore, governments have to improve access to e-democracy opportunities in order to close the gap. Another common belief is that by extending accessibility to high-speed access governments can build social capital online.[36]

According to Bridges.org, which published *Spanning the Digital Divide*, it is difficult to gain an overall understanding of the problem and the possible different solutions to it.[37] At the macro level, there is consensus that economic growth and social equity are both needed to bridge international and domestic digital divides. However, no consensus exists on exactly what policies are needed to achieve either of these goals. Governments face diversified constituencies which hold different opinions on how to bridge the divides. There are those that believe that governments have to regulate policies, whereas others think that free market competition will provide better and more reasonable access. The next section examines the general policies and initiations that are considered relevant in bridging digital divides nationally and internationally, and the preferred policies that will close the digital gap between people with disabilities and the rest of society.

---

[35] Alexandra Samuel, 'From digital divide to digital democracy: Strategies from the community networking movement and beyond', paper presented at the Prospects for Electronic Democracy Conference, Carnegie Mellon University, Pittsburgh, Pennsylvania, 20–22 September 2002.

[36] See, for example M. Jae Moon, 'The evolution of e-government among municipalities: Rhetoric or reality', *Public Administration Review* 62 (2002), 424–33.

[37] The report can be accessed at http://www.bridges.org/publications.

NATIONAL POLICIES TO BRIDGE THE DIGITAL DIVIDE

The United States

The most significant U.S. report about the status of the digital divide is the Pew Research Center's *Internet & American Life Project*, which is aimed at providing in-depth knowledge on Internet access and usage.[38] In order to close the digital divide, the United States has developed different types of policies at federal, state and local levels. These efforts also include public and private sector participation. Policies to close the digital divide and reduce digital literacy in the United States are based on the participation of a mix of government and private sectors.

An Opportunity Nation report published by the U.S. Advisory Council on the national information infrastructure provided the national plan to close the digital divide.[39] The report offered the development of three strategies to deal with disparities in access: (1) information superhighway deployment that can be achieved by removing regulatory disincentives and promoting neutral competitiveness; (2) universal access and service by providing opportunities to producers of information for individuals; and (3) a governmental role in leading and protecting the existence of information and services.[40] This is a generic approach that does not differentiate between subpopulations, including those with disabilities.

The Development of Digital Infrastructure in the United States

The development of digital infrastructure in the United States is remarkable. In 1995, Vice President Al Gore announced the development of a national information infrastructure as a priority of the Clinton administration.[41] Five years later, President Bill Clinton proposed $2.25 billion worth of initiatives to bridge the digital divide, including allocations to encourage private-sector donations of computers, sponsorship

---

[38] Can be accessed at http://www.pewinternet.org/.
[39] *United States Advisory Council on the National Information Infrastructure, 1996. A nation of opportunity: Final report.* Can be accessed at http://www.benton.org/KickStart/nation.home. html.
[40] *United States Advisory Council on the National Information Infrastructure, 1996*, p. 11.
[41] See Sarah Miles, 'A man, a plan, a challenge', *Wired*, 30 January 1998, accessed 12 December 2011 at http://www.wired.com/politics/law/news/1998/01/9939.

of community technology centres and technology training for workers. A budget of $45 million was allocated to promote innovative applications of information and communications technology for underserved communities. However, the major efforts apparently come from the public and private sectors. Large information technology businesses such as Hewlett-Packard, 3Com, Intel, Lucent Technology and Microsoft have played major roles in providing computers and Internet access.[42]

An additional component is the development of networking and connectivity. The Universal Service section in the Telecommunication Act of 1996 was based on the early Communications Act of 1934. The principles of this section were originally to provide quality services at reasonable and affordable rates, equitably and with non-discriminatory contribution to all regions of the United States, as well as emphasising low-income and rural Americans and certain public providers.

The most important section (h-1-B), regulates and facilitates telecommunication services to elementary schools, secondary schools and libraries for educational purposes by providing for lower rates than those charged for similar services to other parties. The Federal Communications Commission responded to that section by setting a maximum-price limitation and discount rates, commonly known as E-rate or education rate, in the Federal-State Joint Board on Universal Service in 1997. The E-rate ruling establishes a matrix for calculating individual discount rates for each eligible school and public library, based on economic status and geographic location. Eligible schools and libraries can earn discounts of 20 to 90 percent on telecommunication services, Internet access and internal connections necessary for deploying technology for educational activities. The Universal Service Fund for schools and libraries has been in place since 1998.

Unfortunately, the Telecommunication Act of 1996, which was intended to provide fairness in competition and remove monopolisation, unintentionally widened the digital divide.[43] The gap is between communities that have adequate and inadequate infrastructures. The solution

---

[42] Songphan Choemprayong, 'Closing digital divides: The United States' policies', *Libri* 56 (2006), 201–12.

[43] Mark Cooper and Gene Kimmelman, 'The digital divide confronts the Telecommunications Act of 1996: Economic Reality Versus Public Policy', the First Triennial Review, February, Consumers Union, 1999. Can be accessed at www.consumersunion.org/pdf/telecom1-0299.pdf.

has included some government regulation through the National Science Foundation (NSF), which initiated a programme called Advanced Networking with Minority-Serving Institutions to protect those who have been denied access.

A number of studies demonstrate how libraries contribute to narrowing the digital divide by offering almost completely free access to computers and the Internet within the poorest communities.[44] However, these positive gains are less relevant to people with disabilities who still experience accessibility and social integration barriers in public domains.

Coping with Digital Illiteracy in the United States

The second strategy by the U.S. federal government was to gradually narrow the gap of digital literacy. The U.S. strategy of closing the literacy gap is due to systematic planning and activities that were initiated in 1987. The American Library Association founded the Presidential Committee on Information Literacy to address information literacy in educational environments, design models for information literacy development and determine implications for the continuing education and development of teachers. In 1999, the Association of College and Research Libraries (ACRL) endorsed the Information Literacy Competency Standards for Higher Education and introduced five key standards as well as performance indicators and expected outcomes.

Remarkable progress was made with the Information Literacy Meeting of Experts, which was conducted in September 2003 and sponsored by the U.S. National Commission on Libraries and Information Science (NCLIS); the National Forum on Information Literacy (NFIL); and the United Nations Education, Scientific and Cultural Organization (UNESCO). The meeting passed the Prague Declaration 'Toward an Information Literacy Society', proposing basic information literacy principles.[45] The declaration includes the following statements:

---

[44] See John C. Bertot, Charles R. McLure and Joe Ryan, 'Impact of external technology funding programs in public libraries: A study of LSTA, e-rate, Gates, and others', *Public Libraries* 41 (2002), 166–71. Accessed at http://www.ala.org/ala//pla/plapubs/publiclibraries/publiclibraries.cfm.

[45] Can be accessed at http://praguedeclaration.org/.

The creation of an Information Society is key to social, cultural and economic development of nations and communities, institutions and individuals in the 21st century and beyond; Information Literacy encompasses knowledge of one's information concerns and needs, and the ability to identify, locate, evaluate, organize and effectively create, use and communicate information to address issues or problems at hand; it is a prerequisite for participating effectively in the Information Society, and is part of the basic human right of lifelong learning; Information Literacy, in conjunction with access to essential information and effective use of information and communication technologies, plays a leading role in reducing the inequities within and among countries and peoples, and in promoting tolerance and mutual understanding through information use in multicultural and multilingual contexts; Governments should develop strong interdisciplinary programs to promote Information Literacy nationwide as a necessary step in closing the digital divide through the creation of an information literate citizenry, an effective civil society and a competitive workforce; Information Literacy is a concern to all sectors of society and should be tailored by each to its specific needs and context; Information Literacy should be an integral part of Education for All, which can contribute critically to the achievement of the United Nations Millennium Development Goals, and respect for the Universal Declaration of Human Rights.

However, these efforts are generic and hardly touch upon information literacy among people with disabilities.

Building a Digital Society in the United States

The third strategy to close the digital gap is the building of digital society. One of the most important goals is to offer digital citizenship by promoting people's participation and engagement. Online national voting was first launched in the United States in 2000.[46] However, it is still a controversial topic and faces opposition and concern in the political system regarding security, integrity and reliability issues.

Another remarkable plan by the Clinton administration was the effort to establish an accessible E-Government system. The Bush

---

[46] In March 2000, the Arizona Democratic Party ran its presidential primary over the Internet using the private company, election.com.

administration announced guidelines for developing an E-Government that is citizen-centred, results-oriented and market-based. The E-Government Act of 2002 was enacted to expand the E-Government initiative.[47] However, in addition to sharing information between government units and providing equal opportunity of access, the act seems to focus more on security issues. In particular, the Federal Information Security Management Act of 2002 responds to the Homeland Security Act.[48]

From the Paper Reduction Act and the first integrated government portal in the Clinton administration,[49] the E-Government initiative has shifted to more trusted and secured standard-based authentication systems. An additional important concept promoted by the federal government is e-commerce. In 1998, Congress created the Advisory Commission on Electronic Commerce to study taxation and tariffs on transactions using the Internet and Internet access on different levels. The commission published its report in 2000 covering six policy areas: sales and use taxes, business activity taxes, Internet access, taxation of telecommunication services and providers, international taxes and tariffs, and the need for improved knowledge of international ramifications.

The digital economy included a digital workforce.[50] A study of the U.S. Department of Commerce pointed out some concerns about the lack of IT professionals in the labour market.[51] The recommendations were introduced in response to digital inequality issues such as increasing and preparing young people to enter technical education and careers, and the participation of groups underrepresented in the technical professions. This is an advanced step in closing the digital divide in the career and professional dimensions, beyond providing basic skills and training services.

However, it seems that despite a body of federal and state laws and policies that promote digital society, there are significant barriers for

---

[47] See the E-Government Act of 2002 (P.L. 107–347, 116 Stat._ 2899, 44 U.S.C.§ 101, H.R. 2458/S. 803.

[48] See the Homeland Security Act (HSA) of 2002, P.L. 107–296, 116 Stat. 745, enacted 25 November 2002.

[49] Firstgov.gov is now available at www.usa.gov.

[50] Choemprayong, 'Closing digital divides'.

[51] An important study carried out by U.S. Department of Commerce, 'Falling through the Net II: New data on the digital divide. National Telecommunications and Information Administration', 1996. Accessed 23 March 2000, http://www.ntia.doc.gov/ntiahome/dn/index.html.

people with disabilities to access when using E-Government and e-commerce. Few of the barriers are technical, but the concern is that people who are socially and economically excluded cannot benefit from the common good. In addition, there are wide variations across states in infrastructure, accessibility and technology.

EUROPE

The situation in Europe is quite similar to that in the United States. A comprehensive policy to reduce the digital divide in Europe was developed by the EU in the second half of the 1990s through the beginning of the new millennium.[52] The two-phase strategy has two goals: (1) economic development and innovation and (2) social inclusion. As with the United States, European policy has been the development of physical access. The EU and its member states prioritised the diffusion of technology and the achievement of physical access to computers and the Internet for as many Europeans as possible.[53] This was enacted by the principles of universal and public access and universal service. In this context, these principles mean that every citizen should either have a private connection to a computer and the Internet preferably at home – but also in educational settings and workplaces (universal access) – or a public connection in a public place such as a library, and public access.

The principle of *universal service* was defined by the European Commission as 'access to a defined minimum service of specified quality to all users independent of their geographical location and, in light of specific national conditions, at an affordable price'.[54] However, unlike in the United States, where the diffusion is based on free market principles, the EU policy is more regulated to ensure the price, quality and geographical availability of services. A large number of obligations forced telecom

---

[52] Jan Van Dijk, 'The digital divide in Europe'. In *The handbook of Internet politics*. Edited by Andrew Chadwick and Philip N. Howard (London: Routledge, 2008). Access at www.utwente.nl/gw/mco/bestanden/digitaldivide.pdf.

[53] Ibid.

[54] The principle of universal service is presented online at the European Commission Site, http://ec.europa.eu/information_society/policy/ecomm/todays_framework/universal_service/index_en.htm.

operators to interconnect their networks, open up their connections for access to the Internet and other digital media by telephone subscribers themselves and provide some public access points.

European policy used additional steps to protect and provide extra resources to disadvantaged groups in Europe, such as hardware and connection cost subsidies to schools in poor neighbourhoods or regions, and additional facilities in public buildings and community access centres. In some European countries, yet another step was taken: to supply hardware, software and training for the unemployed to increase their chances in the labour market.

The second policy phase was emphasising skills, usage and motivational access. In the action plan 'e-Europe 2005: An information society for all',[55] the primary goal was the development of broadband infrastructure, new services and content. However, the policy paid attention to social inclusion by allocating resources to provide skills for adults beyond the education system. In 2005, the EU announced the *i*2010 programme that could be framed as a new digital divide policy: 'In *i*2010 strong emphasis is given to full participation and to providing people with basic digital competence'.[56]

This new policy was summarised in the Riga Declaration of 2006.[57] The background of the policy shift was explained in a 2007 working document: 'It focused on three facets of *e-inclusion*: the access divide (or "early digital divide") which considers the gap between those with and without access; the usage divide ("primary digital divide") concentrating on those who have access but are non-users; and the divide stemming from quality of use ("secondary digital divide") focusing on differentials in participation rates of those people who have access and are users'.

The Riga Declaration focused on six broad policy areas for inclusion:

1. Older workers and elderly people
2. The geographical digital divide

---

[55] e-Europe 2005: An information society for all. An action plan, prepared on 28 May 2002 by European Dynamics SA, Belgium. The e-Europe 2005 Action Plan was agreed at the Seville European Council on 21–22 June 2002 and endorsed by the Council of Ministers in the e-Europe Resolution of January 2003. Can be accessed at http://ec.europa.eu/information_society/eeurope/2005/all_about/action_plan/index_en.htm.

[56] Van Dijk, 'The digital divide in Europe'.

[57] Riga Declaration of 2006, accessed 4 December 2011, http://ec.europa.eu/information_society/events/ict_riga_2006/index_en.htm.

3. E-accessibility and usability
4. Digital literacy
5. Cultural diversity in relation to inclusion
6. Inclusive E-Government

The Riga Declaration was clearly geared toward vulnerable subpopulations such as older people, people with disabilities, women, lower education groups, the unemployed and people in 'less-developed' regions. There is no doubt that this new policy shifted the attention from physical access to skills and usage access, stressing digital literacy and applications that enable people to participate in the information society. In addition, the new policy shifted the focus from the general policy of universal access and service to a much more focused approach for particular social categories and European regions that lagged behind.

The EU recognised that the above resolutions were not enough and therefore the EU Parliament passed a new resolution on the European Disability Strategy 2010–2020.[58] It calls on the European Commission to reinforce antidiscrimination and accessibility provisions in the EU's cohesion policy plans for 2014–2020, public procurement reform proposals and to present a legislative proposal for a European Accessibility Act with strong and binding measures at the EU level to improve access to goods and services for people with disabilities.

CLOSING THE GAP BASED ON EVIDENCE-BASED PRACTICES

A different approach, based on evidence-based practices, has been offered by Heike Boeltzig and Doria Pilling from the IBM Center for the Business of Government.[59] The authors published a report 'Bridging the Digital Divide for Hard-to-Reach Groups'. In their report, Boeltzig and Pilling presented twelve comparative initiatives (six in the United States and six in the UK) geared toward specific groups of people who are typically not connected to the Internet and then examined the circumstances of each – rural, poor, people with disabilities, seniors and ethnic

---

[58] Accessed 4 December 2011, http://eur-lex.europa.eu/LexUriServ/LexUriServ.do?uri=COM:2010:0636:FIN:EN:PDF.

[59] The report was published by Heike Boeltzig and Doria Pilling in 2007 and can be accessed at www.communityinclusion.org/pdf/digitaldivide.pdf.

minorities. They focused on how these groups of people, such as home-bound individuals, could benefit most from using online government services. They also identified technical as well as social barriers that limit access.

Based on their comparative projects in the United States and the UK, they offered ten recommendations to increase access and use for these targeted groups.[60]

RECOMMENDATIONS FOR INCREASING ACCESS

1. Provide free computer and Internet access to targeted groups
2. Provide long-term support to organisations seeking to reach targeted groups
3. Create partnerships with other organisations to share resources and expertise
4. Create strategies for long-term project sustainability

RECOMMENDATIONS FOR INCREASING USE

1. Engage individuals' interests and concerns
2. Raise awareness and benefits of E-Government services
3. Improve usability of the Internet and E-Government services
4. Improve computer and Internet 'accessibility'
5. Create a comfortable learning environment and provide informal training opportunities
6. Involve targeted users through ongoing consultation

CONCLUSION

It is evident that socioeconomic and legal strategies can be meaningful if the societal climate supports the inclusion of people with disabilities. In addition, the digital revolution can be a vehicle for change if people

---

[60] Ibid.; Boeltzig and Pilling, p. 13.

with disabilities can enjoy access and the use of new technologies. This chapter introduced and analysed national and international strategies for change and promotion of positive and acceptable portrayals in the printed and digital media. In addition, it presented and discussed barriers to and strategies for narrowing the digital divide.

Interestingly, the best-known macro strategies for changing negative media images are guidelines for adequate portrayals of people with disabilities in the media and increasing Web accessibility. The strategies' shortcoming is compliance by writers, producers and others in the media. The second macro strategy of adoption of Article 8 (raising awareness) of the UN CRPD has the potential to be the road map. However, the main problem is transforming the article to domestic policies. The third strategy used primarily in Europe and Australia is domestic media campaigns and projects designed to increase and improve the portrayal of people with disabilities in the media. These campaigns are visible but limited in impact and scope.

There are micro-strategies that tend to touch upon specific sub-populations or issues. The best-known programme that has been shown to raise children's awareness of disabilities is *The Kids on the Block*. This educational programme was one of the most cited and successful interventions to change attitudes of children at an early age. Additional micro projects include progressive advertising and recognising successful media practices; however, these are limited in scope and impact.

The second part of this chapter provided an in-depth review and analysis of the strategies that will bridge the digital divide for people with disabilities. It focuses primarily on the United States and Europe, and documents solutions for bridging the gap. The common approach held by governments is technological and expects that people, including those with disabilities, will benefit from this development. In contrast, however, social scientists and policy makers argue that the focus should be on people, their developmental needs, issues of poverty and lack of social-techno access. A pragmatic approach, presented at the end of this chapter, provides evidence-based practices in addition to several recommendations for increasing access and use for targeted vulnerable groups.

9   CLOSING REMARKS

In the closing remarks, I would like to highlight and respond briefly to core questions related to social inclusion for people with disabilities nationally and internationally. What is the impact of biblical, theological and historical perspectives on current views of inclusion of people with disabilities? Which strategy – social or legal – is more effective in promoting social inclusion of people with disabilities? Can the media change portrayals of people with disabilities? Is it possible to narrow the digital divide?

WHAT ARE THE IMPACTS OF BIBLICAL, THEOLOGICAL AND HISTORICAL PERSPECTIVES ON THE CURRENT VIEWS OF INCLUSION?

Chapter 2 discusses theological views on people with disabilities as they appear in the Bible, the New Testament and the Qur'an. Christian theology identifies three controversial themes that may reflect barriers toward inclusion of people with disabilities in society.[1] The first theme associates disability with sin and the belief that the sin is a punishment for wrongdoing, which therefore justifies social exclusion. The second theme links disability to suffering and recognises the endurance and passive acceptance of the marginalised role. The third theme identifies the disabled person as an object of charity, in need of support but remote from public eye.

Jewish theology adopts a dualistic approach toward the ability of people with disabilities to be integrated into society. Leviticus, the third

---

[1] Nancy L. Eisland, *The disabled God: Toward a liberatory theology of disability* (Nashville, TN: Abingdon Press, 1994).

book of the Torah, calls for compassion and protection of people who are deaf and blind by commanding 'Thou shalt not curse the deaf nor put a stumbling block before the blind, nor maketh the blind to wander out of path'.[2] However, in the same book, people with disabilities are considered not fit or pure enough to serve as priests in the Temple: 'The Lord spoke further to Moses: Speak to Aaron and say: No man of your offspring throughout the ages who has a defect shall be qualified to offer the food of his God'.[3] Given the centrality of religion in some peoples' lives, it is important to lead a theological dialogue about modern interpretation of disability in spiritual life. The Qur'an does not relate to specific disabilities and interprets disability as a social deprivation issue.

There are many historical traces of disability that are still evident in our time. Most of the attitudes toward people with disabilities are rooted in the ancient, medieval and early modern periods. They depict images of people with disabilities as sinners who are also in need of compassion; mercy stems from the Bible and the New Testament. The idea and practice of infanticide are based on Aristotelian views of the human body in Ancient Greece, or the demonology and witchcraft beliefs of the Middle Ages.

The role of history is not limited to portrayals of disability. In his book *A History of Disability*, Stiker argues that modern interpretations of terms such as 'assimilation', 'integration' and 'inclusion' are rooted in the history of mankind.[4] Our progressive legislation is imbedded in Early Roman Law, such as the concept of guardianship or the Justinian Code which classified persons with disabilities by their severity.[5] They became the infrastructure of law in most European countries from the sixth to the eighteenth century.

However, history also teaches us about the negative concepts and practices that were harmful to people with disabilities, such as the eugenic sterilisation laws that were prevalent in the United States at the beginning of the twentieth century, and the sterilisation and euthanasia laws and practices carried out in Nazi Germany before and during World War II.

[2] Lev., 19, 4.
[3] Lev., 21:16–20.
[4] Stiker, *A history of disability*, p. 13.
[5] Catherine J. Kudlick, 'Disability history', *The American Historical Review* 108 (2003), 766.

Finally, history provides an insightful look at the rise of institutional-isation in the Western world, and shows that their expansion in response to overwhelming social and economic changes leads to social exclusion, benign neglect and violation of human rights.

Much of the new research on the role of history in shaping our modern legislation, policies and practices came from disability studies.[6] Those scholars who interpreted the history of disability in social, political and cultural terms rather than individualistic terms gave it a different meaning. For political and policy historians, disability is central to the development of the modern state by challenging issues such as social protection, social assistance and citizenship.[7] Similarly, labour historians may challenge issues and norms of productivity and inclusion in the workforce. If modern society strives to move toward social inclusion policies, it must use history as an analytic tool alongside social, economical and legal ones.

WHICH STRATEGY IS MORE EFFECTIVE IN PROMOTING SOCIAL INCLUSION OF PEOPLE WITH DISABILITIES?

Social protection and human rights strategies toward social inclusion of people with disabilities are often described as competitive approaches. Social protection instruments are considered as traditional and are common in most Western countries. Disability rights legislation is a fairly new strategy that has been added to the infrastructure of social protection provisions. Do the two core strategies stand one against the other? Or are they complementary and can they be merged into one unified policy?

Both strategies are geared toward the reduction of social exclusion of people with disabilities, in particular promoting their participation in the labour force and civic society. However, their paths are quite different: Social protection is considered the frontline at which European-regulated policy aims to beat social exclusion related to poverty, unemployment and certain norms of social, economic or political activity applying to

---

[6] Ibid., 765.
[7] Ibid., 766.

individuals, households, spatial areas or population groups. The American approach is characterised by lesser government regulation and reduced social protection provisions.

If the social protection and social capital strategies are more common in Europe than in the United States, it seems that the human rights approach was initiated and is more prevalent in the United States. The ADA enacted in 1990 extends similar civil rights to people with disabilities that other groups already have had on the basis of race, sex, national origin and religion. The model rejects the premise that social exclusion is inevitably the consequence of disability and posits that the failure to accommodate people with disabilities in society is discrimination.[8] Under the civil rights model, the goal of disability policy is to use legal intervention in order to ensure that people with disabilities will not be excluded from society. Europe, as well as other countries, has enacted similar disability rights legislation in addition to the existing social protection provisions.

There are significant differences between the social protection and human rights strategies that stem from different perspectives: the first is predominantly a social protection policy that inherited the medical and social welfare models, whereas the second, the human rights model, is basically an antidiscrimination tool geared toward social participation.[9] However, most of the Western nations' policies contain a mixture of the two.

However, it is unclear how social welfare or social assistance programmes that require means testing and the provision of separate services and facilities for people with severe disabilities can operate alongside antidiscrimination legislation, which intervenes against separate services.

States tend to solve these contradictions by adjusting current policies to prevailing antidiscrimination legislations. For example, they may change income support programmes or eliminate quotas in employment

[8] See Joseph P. Shapiro, *No pity: People with disabilities forging a new civil rights movement* (New York: Times Books, 1993).

[9] Lisa Waddington and Mathew Diller, 'Tensions and coherence in disability policy: The uneasy relationship between social welfare and civil rights models of disability in American, European, and international employment law'. In *Disability rights law and policy: International and national perspectives*. Edited by Mary Lou Breslin and Silvia Yee (New York: Transnational Publishers, 2002), pp. 241–82.

policies. Nevertheless, there is a recognition that the human rights approach cannot address all the demonstrated needs of people with disabilities. There are two suggestions as to how states can bridge the two strategies. The first recommendation is to broaden the concept of civil rights beyond antidiscrimination conceptualisation and to adopt equality as the core principle for social protection policies. The second recommendation is to transform social welfare to the social justice model, meaning that the focus of government policy is to remove barriers in the labour market and in society as a whole in order to promote economic and social participation.

The newest international effort to provide both strategies – human rights and social protection – is the UN CRPD. This comprehensive international instrument has two layers. The first is protection of rights such as expression of speech, thought, religion and political participation. The second is actually the provision of adequate standards of living. It is interesting that beyond the human rights' articles, the convention includes typical social strategies such as Articles 27 and 28. Article 27 emphasises the rights of persons with disabilities to work on an equal basis with others, including their right to equal pay for equal work and trade union rights. Article 28 provides adequate standards of living and social protection such as food and housing, social security and poverty alleviation schemes. However, as with the implementation of any social policy, the challenge is whether it can be translated from declarative and abstract rights to domestic law with substantial results.

CAN THE MEDIA CHANGE PORTRAYALS OF PEOPLE WITH DISABILITIES AND IS IT POSSIBLE TO NARROW THE DIGITAL DIVIDE?

Chapters 4 and 8 demonstrate that the media has an extremely important role in facilitating the exclusion or integration of people with disabilities. The media leads popular culture, stereotypes, language and social trends, and, as such, depicts and also underrepresents people with disabilities. The impression is that in recent years there is a recognition that the media has to present a more balanced and progressive image of people with disabilities. This is evident in Article 8 of the UN CRPD, which calls for raising awareness. There are documented strategies to promote positive and acceptable portrayals in the printed and digital media.

The easiest strategy to change stereotypes in the media is to set guidelines for adequately portraying people with disabilities in the printed and digital media and to ensure Web accessibility. However, the media is free and the guidelines are only suggestions that cannot be enforced. In fact, imposing rules stands against the media's nature to capture the audience and sell in order to be profitable.

The use of media campaigns, primarily in Europe and Australia, is important in raising awareness, but is limited in scope. Surprisingly, the most promising are the micro-strategies that tend to touch upon specific subpopulations or issues. An effective way to raise children's awareness of disabilities was the *Kids on the Block* educational programme. However, it seems that future efforts have to be directed toward the new media's impact on people with disabilities. It is a more interactive and egalitarian media that requires active participation on the part of people with disabilities.

The new media raises problems of accessibility and usability for people with disabilities. Policies adopted in the United States and Europe have demonstrated that there has been remarkable progress in digital infrastructure and social-techno access. However, although people with disabilities have gained significantly from the digital revolution, their progress lags in comparison to those without disabilities. Therefore, governments need to adopt comprehensive policies and plans that provide accessible, usable and intelligent resources on a larger scale than we see today.

POSTSCRIPT

A salient and important component related to social inclusion of persons with disabilities is the family. In addition to significant others and care givers, the family plays the pivotal role in providing stability, supports, socialization and opportunities for social inclusion. As has been discussed, since the early 1990s, there has been a significant change in disability policies in the United States, Europe and other Western countries, from medical and social welfare legislations to social-functional and human rights. One of the core questions is whether this transition has incorporated needs and concerns raised by families of persons with disabilities, particularly as family caregivers age and people with disabilities live longer.

My forthcoming book, *Family Policy and Disability*, examines comparatively and in particular national and international family policies toward disability. The book continues the discussion began in this project regarding the critical role of family supports to the success of the UNCRPD. It also explores those modifications that may be required by countries to adapt progressive family disability policies for the promotion of human rights and the inclusion of persons with disabilities in society in the coming years.

INDEX

Made in the USA
Middletown, DE
18 May 2015